MW00885372

History is a treasure chest of stories, waiting to be opened by curious minds.

Think of history as the world's biggest classroom; there's always something new to learn!

YOUR NAME:

AGE:

SCHOOL:

Pearl Harbor: A Day of Infamy

"Attention all hands on deck!" Imagine hearing this urgent call echo across the naval base at Pearl Harbor, Hawaii, on the morning of December 7, 1941. It was a sunny Sunday like any other, with sailors and soldiers enjoying their morning routines, when suddenly, the sky darkened with aircraft. This was no drill — the United States Naval Base at Pearl Harbor was under attack by the Imperial Japanese Navy Air Service.

The peaceful waters churned violently as torpedoes sliced through, aimed at the heart of the American Pacific Fleet. Battleships like the USS Arizona and the USS Oklahoma became targets of a surprise attack that was as strategic as it was devastating. In just two hours, the Japanese managed to damage or destroy 20 American naval vessels, including eight enormous battleships, and over 300 airplanes. The tranquil paradise of Hawaii was transformed into a landscape of billowing smoke and fiery destruction.

This attack was not just a military strike; it was a moment that changed the course of history. Before the attack, the United States had been hesitant to join World War II, which had been raging in Europe and Asia. But with the fall of Pearl Harbor, the nation was galvanized into action. The following day, President Franklin D. Roosevelt addressed the nation, calling December 7th "a date which will live in infamy." The United States declared war on Japan, officially entering World War II — a war that would span the globe and define an era.

Pearl Harbor taught the nation a valuable lesson about preparedness and the importance of being vigilant in a world where conflict could arise suddenly and without warning. It's a day to remember the lives lost, the heroes who emerged, and the spirit of unity that rose from the ashes.

Multiple Choice Questions:

1. What was targeted during the attack on Pearl Harbor?

- A) The entire island of Hawaii	- B) American naval vessels and airplanes	- C) Commercial cargo ships

2. How did the United States respond to the attack on Pearl Harbor?

- A) By signing a peace treaty with Japan	- B) By declaring war on Japan	- C) By asking for an apology from Japan

3. Which ship became a symbol of the devastating attack and a memorial to this day?

- A) USS Enterprise	- B) USS Missouri	- C) USS Arizona

4. How long did the attack on Pearl Harbor last?

- A) Two days	- B) Two hours	- C) One week

5. What was the immediate effect of the attack on Pearl Harbor in terms of U.S. involvement in World War II?

- A) It caused the U.S. to remain neutral	- B) It led to the U.S. declaring war on Japan and entering World War II	- C) It had no effect on U.S. foreign policy

Julius Caesar, Roman Dictator

Julius Caesar played a big part in the rise of the Roman Empire and made social and governmental changes. Caesar was not a noble when he was born in Rome, Italy, in July of 100 BC. His parents were not powerful people in politics, and they were not rich. Caesar's story of how he went from being a low-class citizen to becoming a Dictator is one of hard work, inspiration, and personal triumph.

The Rome of Caesar's youth was not stable at all. A few years after leaving Rome and joining the military, Caesar returned to Rome to get involved in politics. This is how it worked: He became a public speaker and advocated for the law. Because of his passionate speech, he was well-known. Most of the time, he spoke out against corrupt politicians. It took a long time, but Caesar was eventually elected to the government office. He started working his way up the political ladder.

He was chosen to be the Chief Priest of the Roman state religion when he was first chosen for the job. Afterward, he was chosen to run Spain in 62 BC. This was a big success. While in Spain, he overthrew two tribes and finished his time there well.

Caesar returned to Rome to run a counsel electoral campaign. During that election, Caesar worked closely with Pompey, a former military officer, and Crassus, one of the wealthiest men in Rome, to help them win. This partnership worked out well for Caesar because it gave him power and money. The First Triumvirate was the name given to the three men because of how close they were.

Caesar was elected easily and made a lot of laws that people liked. He was chosen to run Northern Italy and parts of southeast Europe in the next step.

The 13 Legione led Caesar to conquer Gaul, now France and Belgium. He also punished his enemies by cutting off their hands to show them that they were not welcome in the city. In the end, Caesar was known for the way he treated his enemies.

In 50 BC, the Senate, led by Pompey, told Caesar to go home because his term as governor had ended, so he had to leave. It took Pompey a long time to change his mind about Caesar, but he did.

Caesar went to war with Pompey. Caesar took over Italy and pushed Pompey into Egypt, where Pompey was killed. When Caesar was in Egypt, he had an affair with Cleopatra, who gave birth to Caesar's only known biological son, Caesarion, born after the affair.

Crassus was defeated and killed in a battle in Syria.

They overthrew their king in 509 BC, who had all the power and could rule without the Senate or citizen votes. A system of checks and balances like the US one was put into place to make sure the new government worked well in Rome, which was democratic at one point. However, the Roman founders also included an "emergency clause" that said that the Senate could vote to give absolute power to one man as a dictator when the country was in trouble. This way, the Senate could have strong leaders to help them get through that time. Many people were talking about war and chaos in Rome by 48 BC. Much political corruption took place. Finally, the Senate agreed that Caesar should be made the new ruler.

During Caesar's time as ruler, he made significant progress for Rome. Caesar changed the debt laws in Rome, which freed up a lot of money for the people. In addition, Caesar changed the Senate and election rules.

Most importantly, Caesar made changes to the Roman calendar. The calendar used to be based on the phases of the moon. There were more months in the calendar in this newly updated Julian Calendar. It was set to have 365 days and had a leap day every four years at the end of February. It's almost the same as the Western calendar we use today.

During his time as dictator, Caesar became more and more interested in power. They were worried that Caesar would not step down as dictator when the time came. Then, Marcus Brutus came up with a plan to kill Caesar on the Ides of March (the 15th) in 44 BC. Caesar was going to be killed at a meeting of the Senate at the Theater of Pompey.

It is thought that 60 or more men were involved. Caesar was stabbed 23 times on the Senate floor, and it is thought that there were more than 60 people involved.

During the years following the death of Caesar, there were five civil wars. These wars helped to form the Roman Empire.

Caesar was swiftly martyred and, two years later, became the first Roman to be worshiped.

When Caesar was alive, he was married three times. He married Cornelia Cinnilla for the first time when he was 18. (married 83 BC - 69 BC.) Afterward, Julia married Pompey and gave birth to a child, but she didn't live long enough to see it grow up. She was his second wife (married 67 BC - 61 BC.) His third wife was Calpurnia Pisonis, and they had a daughter together (married 59 BC - 44 BC.) Caesar had an affair with Cleopatra, which led to a son named Caesarion. Since it was an extramarital relationship, Caesarion was never recognized as Caesar's son by the Roman government.

Caesar named his great-nephew Octavian in his will. Octavian became the first Roman emperor, Augustus Caesar, in the end.

1. **Caesar made changes to the Roman ____.**
   a. history
   b. calendar

2. **Julius Caesar parents were the most powerful people in politics.**
   a. True
   b. False

3. **Julius Caesar became a public speaker and advocated for the ____.**
   a. government
   b. law

4. **Julius was chosen to run Spain in ____ BC**
   a. 62
   b. 32

5. **Caesar worked closely with ____, a former military officer, and ____, one of the wealthiest men in Rome**
   a. Crassus, Poindexter
   b. Pompey, Crassus

6. **Caesar changed the debt laws in ___.**
   a. Rome
   b. Egypt

7. **____ came up with a plan to kill Caesar on the Ides of March.**
   a. Marcus Brutus
   b. Mark Buccaning

8. **What wars helped to form the Roman Empire?**
   a. civil wars
   b. World War II

The Thirteen Colonies

In 1776, thirteen British colonies merged to form the United States. Many of these colonies had existed for well over a century, including Virginia's first colony, founded in 1607.

A colony is a region of land that is politically controlled by another country. As was the case with England and the American colonies, the controlling country is usually physically distant from the colony. Colonies are typically founded and settled by people from the home country, but settlers from other countries may also be present. This was especially true of the American colonies, which people from all over Europe populated.

Here is a list of the thirteen colonies, along with the year they were established and a description of how they were established.

Virginia: John Smith and the London Company set out for Virginia in 1607.

New York: The Dutch founded New York in 1626. In 1664, it became a British colony.

New Hampshire: John Mason was the first landholder in New Hampshire (1623). Eventually, John Wheelwright.

Massachusetts Bay: Puritans seeking religious freedom in Massachusetts Bay (1630).

Maryland (1633) - George and Cecil Calvert established it as a safe haven for Catholics.

Connecticut (1636) - Thomas Hooker, who had been ordered to leave Massachusetts.

Rhode Island: Roger Williams founded Rhode Island (1636) to provide a place of religious freedom for all.

Delaware: Peter Minuit and the New Sweden Company founded Delaware in 1638. In 1664, the British took over.

North Carolina (1663) - Originally a part of the Carolina Province. Separated from South Carolina in 1712.

South Carolina (1663) - Originally a part of the Carolina Province. In 1712, South Carolina seceded from North Carolina. **New**

Jersey (1664) - Initially settled by the Dutch, the English took control in 1664.

Pennsylvania (1681) William Penn and the Quakers.

Georgia (1732) - James Oglethorpe as a debtor's settlement.

Queen Elizabeth desired to establish colonies in the Americas to expand the British Empire and compete with the Spanish. The English hoped to find riches, create new jobs, and develop trade ports along the Americas' coasts.

Each colony, on the other hand, has its distinct history of how it was founded. Many of the colonies were established by religious leaders or groups seeking religious liberty. Pennsylvania, Massachusetts, Maryland, Rhode Island, and Connecticut were among these colonies. Other colonies were established solely to create new trade opportunities and profits for investors.

The colonies are frequently divided into New England Colonies, Middle Colonies, and Southern Colonies.

New England Colonies: Connecticut, Massachusetts Bay, New Hampshire, Rhode Island

Middle Colonies: Delaware, New Jersey, New York, Pennsylvania

Southern Colonies: Georgia, Maryland, North Carolina, South Carolina, Virginia

1. **The Dutch founded _____ in 1626.**
    a. New Jersey
    b. New York

2. **13 British colonies merged to form the_____.**
    a. United Kingdom
    b. United States

3. **Roger Williams founded _____.**
    a. Maryland
    b. Rhode Island

4. **A colony is a region of _____ that is politically controlled by another country.**
    a. land
    b. township

5. **Middle Colonies:**
    a. Delaware, New Jersey, New York, Pennsylvania
    b. Georgia, Maryland, North Carolina, South Carolina, Texas

6. **Colonies are typically founded and settled by people from the ___ country.**
    a. home
    b. outside

7. **Southern Colonies:**
    a. Maine, New Jersey, New York, Pennsylvania
    b. Georgia, Maryland, North Carolina, South Carolina, Virginia

8. **Many of the colonies were established by _____ leaders or groups seeking religious liberty.**
    a. political
    b. religious

9. **New England Colonies:**
    a. Connecticut, Massachusetts Bay, New Hampshire, Rhode Island
    b. Ohio, Tennessee, New York, Pennsylvania

10. **George and Cecil Calvert established _____ as a safe haven for Catholics.**
    a. Maine
    b. Maryland

11. **The colonies are frequently divided into_____.**
    a. New England Colonies, Middle Colonies, and Southern Colonies
    b. United England Colonies, Midland Colonies, and Southern Colonies.

Amazon Rainforest Fires: A Global Call to Action

First, read all the way through. After that, go back and fill in the blanks. You can skip the blanks you're unsure about and finish them later.

forest	trees	park	nature	cows
health	blackout	South	dioxide	humans

Deep in the heart of _____ America lies a green giant named the Amazon Rainforest. But recently, this gentle giant has been facing some heated trouble, quite literally. Imagine if your local _____ started bursting into flames, and now imagine that park being millions of acres large - that's what's happening in the Amazon!

The Amazon isn't just any _____. It's often called the 'lungs of the Earth' because it breathes in carbon _____ and breathes out fresh, clean oxygen. In fact, it provides 20% of the world's oxygen. That's a lot of heavy breathing!

So, when fires began roaring across the Amazon, it wasn't just the toucans and jaguars that were alarmed. The entire world sat up and took notice. The smokey air traveled across countries, even causing a daytime _____ in São Paulo, Brazil!

But here's the thing - while some fires are natural, many of these fires are started deliberately by _____. Why? Well, for things like farming and mining. The idea is that if there's no forest, there's more room for _____ and crops. But at what cost?

The world rallied together, with young and old voicing their concerns. Protests, fundraisers, and global meetings were organized, and it became clear: The Amazon's _____ is everyone's responsibility.

This fiery issue isn't just about _____. It's about balancing human needs with the health of our planet. The Amazon fires have shown that when _____ sends an SOS, it's a call for all of us to spring into action!

American History Fill-in-Blank

Score: _____

Date: _____

American history is a tale of progress, resilience, and hope. From the early pioneers to the civil rights movement, Americans have shown courage and determination in the face of adversity in order to make this country great. Whether it was fighting for freedom or pushing back against oppressive forces, Americans have consistently stood up for what they believe and created a more perfect union. This spirit of perseverance and innovation has shaped our nation's diverse cultural identity and continues to inspire generations today.

Through hard work, dedication, and an unyielding determination to succeed, they were able to carve out a place in an unknown land and create a nation that stands as a beacon of hope and progress today. From the American Revolution to emancipation and civil rights, Americans have drawn on their resilience to fight for what's right in order to advance their society. This dogged attitude has profoundly impacted American culture, inspiring creativity and innovation in all aspects of life—from art to technology—which reflects our open-minded outlook towards change and growth.

_____

During this exercise, you will fill in the blanks with the correct word to match their definitions or clues. Need help? Try Google.

technique	indigenous	amenable	analogous	laudable
beliefs	ascertain	avarice	kinship	mission

1. She adhered to her own _____ and would not accede to the demands of others.

2. The _____ language was lost as settlers moved into the area.

3. He was _____ to the suggestions put forward and made changes accordingly.

4. His ire was quickly raised when she suggested he had failed in his _____.

5. They sought to _____ the truth behind what had happened before making any decisions.

6. The juxtaposition of the two paintings highlighted their stark contrast in style and _____.

7. Their approach to business was _____ to how they handled their personal lives, calm and collected, no matter what curveballs were thrown their way.

8. Despite having no blood relation, they felt a strong sense of _____ with one another due to their shared experiences and interests over many years together.

9. He was consumed by _____ and constantly sought out more wealth at any cost, even at the expense of his own health.

10. Her work stood out from the rest, and its excellence was _____ in every respect.

Christopher Columbus

When Christopher Columbus discovered America, he set in motion centuries of transatlantic colonization. He was an Italian explorer.

Christopher Columbus made four trips across the Atlantic Ocean from Spain in 1492, 1493, 1498, and 1502. He was adamant about finding a direct water route west from Europe to Asia, but he never succeeded. Instead, he discovered the Americas. Though he did not "discover" the so-called New World—millions of people already lived there—his voyages marked the start of centuries of exploration and colonization of North and South America.

With three ships: the Nina, the Pinta, and the Santa Maria, Columbus, and his crew set sail from Spain on August 3, 1492. The ships arrived in the Bahamas on October 12, not in the East Indies, as Columbus had assumed, but on one of the Bahamian islands, most likely San Salvador.

Columbus sailed from island to island in what is now known as the Caribbean for months, looking for the "pearls, precious stones, gold, silver, spices, and other objects and merchandise whatsoever" that he had promised his Spanish patrons, but he didn't find much. In January 1493, he set sail for Spain, leaving several dozen men behind in a makeshift settlement on Hispaniola (present-day Haiti and the Dominican Republic).

During his first voyage, he kept a detailed diary. Christopher Columbus' journal was written between August 3, 1492, and November 6, 1492, and it describes everything from the wildlife he saw, such as dolphins and birds, to the weather and the moods of his crew.

Circle the correctly spelled word.

	A	B	C	D
1.	America	Amerryca	Ameryca	Amerrica
2.	spices	spicesc	spises	spicess
3.	Eurropaen	European	Europaen	Eurropean
4.	coast	coasct	cuast	coasst
5.	abrroad	abruad	abroad	abrruad
6.	sailor	siallor	saillor	sialor
7.	nations	nattions	nascons	natsions
8.	explurers	explorers	expllorers	expllurers
9.	sylver	syllver	sillver	silver
10.	Spayn	Spian	Spyan	Spain
11.	Indains	Indainss	Indianss	Indians
12.	discover	disssover	disscover	dissover
13.	islend	iscland	island	issland

Darius the Great

ruler	storm	Battle	carved	army
famous	happy	experience	Middle	led

Many stories have appeared on the news about conflicts in the _____ East from Egypt to Iran. Do you think you have what it takes to lead this area of the country? It's a difficult challenge, but 2500 years ago, a single person ruled over this entire region and dealt with its issues. The Middle East was once a part of a vast region known as the Persian Empire. Darius the Great, the Persian Empire's most _____ ruler, ruled during the empire's height of power and size.

The Behistun Inscription, which means writing, has revealed much about Darius' life. Darius had his biography and accomplishments _____ into the face of a mountain for them to be remembered and respected. According to the Inscription, Darius was the son of a Persian nobleman, but not the son of the previous emperor. Darius overthrew the emperor's son and became the new _____ of Persia with the assistance of six other nobles.

In order to maintain control, Darius had to devote time to fighting rebellions. After destroying his last known enemies, he considered expanding his kingdom. Darius began by joining parts of northern India. Following that, he _____ his army into Scythia, the northern part of the Black Sea and a vital trading region.

Afterward, the Persian Empire stretched from Europe to the Indian Ocean, making it one of the largest empires. Darius may have ruled over up to half of humanity. He is renowned for decorating his palace hall with images of _____ people throughout the empire rather than conflict and war. However, he went one step further by choosing to fight the Greeks.

The Greeks and Persians had never gotten along, but both had left the other alone for much of their history. On the other hand, Darius desired to combine Greece into his empire. A protest or retaliation against the Persians took place among the Greeks who lived in modern-day Turkey. Darius attempted to make peace with the Greeks at first but ultimately decided it would be easier to conquer them with his gigantic _____. There were two main goals for Darius: punish the Greek leaders of the rebels and seize as many Greek cities as possible.

At first, Darius and the Persians won a series of minor victories over the Greeks, conquering cities and many of Greece's islands, and believed they could beat the rest of the region. However, he began to _____ significant difficulties. The first was a massive _____ that destroyed 200 of his ships and possibly 30,000 of his soldiers.

Following that, Darius' army fought and lost against the Greeks at the _____ of Marathon. The 26-mile race is named after this battle because a messenger ran the distance to Athens to announce the Persian defeat. The Battle of Marathon did not end the Greek-Persian wars, but Darius died shortly afterward, and his son Xerxes took over the war.

Fabulous Age of Technology:
From Phones to Drones

Once upon a techy time, not so very long ago, humanity embarked on an electrifying journey into the dazzling world of gadgets and gizmos. This story begins with the humble cell phone, which transformed from a brick-like contraption to a magical screen we simply cannot live without!

Picture it: The early 2000s. People are wandering around, flipping open their cell phones, unaware that a revolution is around the corner. Enter smartphones! Suddenly, the world had a device that was part phone, part computer, part camera, and entirely mesmerizing. With the rise of smartphones came apps for everything: taking photos, ordering food, playing games, and even for learning languages or playing virtual pianos!

As people got used to having a mini-computer in their pockets, the tech world threw another surprise: the rise of social media. Platforms like Facebook, Instagram, and Twitter became the new hangout spots. Sharing selfies, tweeting thoughts, and watching videos of cute cats became a part of daily life.

But why stop at phones? The skies were soon buzzing with drones. These flying robots, initially used for military purposes, became popular for filming breathtaking aerial views. Movie directors no longer needed helicopters for aerial shots; drones did the job! And it wasn't long before drones started delivering packages right to people's doorsteps.

Now, imagine this: You're walking around your city, and you see cars without drivers. Sounds like a scene from a sci-fi movie, right? Wrong! Self-driving cars, powered by intricate algorithms and sensors, started cruising down real roads, making the idea of a 'futuristic city' seem more present than future.

The climax of our story is the virtual world. Virtual Reality (VR) and Augmented Reality (AR) headsets whisked people away to new dimensions. With VR, one could dive deep into oceans, scale tall mountains, or dance on the moon, all from the comfort of their living room.

So, as our techy tale winds down, one can't help but wonder: what's next? Only time will tell, but one thing is for sure: the future is bound to be electrifying!

True or False Questions:

1. The first cell phones were sleek and slim. _____

2. Smartphones can only be used for making calls and sending texts. _____

3. Drones were initially designed for creating movies. _____

4. Self-driving cars are operated by human drivers using remote controls. _____

5. With Virtual Reality, you can experience new dimensions without leaving your home. _____

6. The story predicts the exact technological advancements of the future. _____

Government History: How Laws Are Made

Congress is the federal government's legislative branch, and it is in charge of making laws for the entire country. Congress is divided into two legislative chambers: the United States Senate and the United States House of Representatives. Anyone elected to either body has the authority to propose new legislation. A bill is a new law proposal.

People living in the United States and its territories are subject to federal laws.

Bills are created and passed by Congress. The president may then sign the bills into law. Federal courts may examine the laws to see if they are in accordance with the Constitution. If a court finds a law to be unconstitutional, it has the authority to overturn it.

The United States government has enacted several laws to help maintain order and protect the country's people. Each new law must be approved by both houses of Congress as well as the President. Before it becomes a new law in the nation, each law must go through a specific process.

The majority of laws in the United States begin as bills. An idea is the starting point for a bill. That thought could come from anyone, including you! The idea must then be written down and explained as the next step. A bill is the name given to the first draft of an idea. The bill must then be sponsored by a member of Congress. The sponsor is someone who strongly supports the bill and wishes to see it become law. A Senator or a member of the House of Representatives can be the sponsor.

The bill is then introduced in either the House or the Senate by the bill's sponsor. Once submitted, the bill is given a number and is officially recorded as a bill.

The bill is assigned to a committee after it is introduced. Committees are smaller groups of congress members who are experts in specific areas. For example, if the bill concerns classroom size in public schools, it would be referred to the Committee on Education. The committee goes over the bill's specifics. They bring in experts from outside Congress to testify and debate the bill's pros and cons.

The committee may decide to make changes to the bill before it is passed. If the committee finally agrees to pass the bill, it will be sent to the House or Senate's main chamber for approval.

If the bill was introduced in the House, it would first be considered by the House. The bill will be discussed and debated by the representatives. House members will then vote on the bill. If the bill is passed, it will be sent to the Senate for consideration.

The Senate will then follow the same procedure. It will discuss and debate the bill before voting. If the Senate approves the bill, it will be sent to the President.

The President's signature is the final step in a bill becoming law. When the President signs the bill, it becomes law.

The President has the option of refusing to sign the bill. This is known as a veto. The Senate and House can choose to override the President's veto by voting again. The bill must now be approved by a two-thirds majority in both the Senate and the House to override the veto.

A bill must be signed into law by the President within 10-days. If he does not sign it within 10-days, one of two things may occur:

1) It will become law if Congress is in session.

2) It will be considered vetoed if Congress is not in session (this is called a pocket veto).

1. If the Senate approves the bill, it will be sent to the _____.
   a. President
   b. House Representee

2. The _____ may decide to make changes to the bill before it is passed.
   a. governor
   b. committee

3. The bill must then be _____ by a member of Congress.
   a. signed
   b. sponsored

4. The President has the option of refusing to sign the bill. This is known as a ___.
   a. voted
   b. veto

5. The Senate and House can choose to override the President's veto by _____again.
   a. creating a new bill
   b. voting

6. The bill is assigned to a committee after it is _____.
   a. introduced
   b. vetoed

7. Bills are created and passed by _____.
   a. The House
   b. Congress

8. A bill must be signed into law by the President within ___-days.
   a. 10
   b. 5

9. The President's _____ is the final step in a bill becoming law.
   a. signature
   b. saying yes

10. If the committee agrees to pass the bill, it will be sent to the House or Senate's main ___ for approval.
    a. chamber
    b. state

Extra Credit: What are some of the weirdest laws in the world? List at least 5.

Historical Figures

First, read all the way through. After that, go back and fill in the blanks. You can skip the blanks you're unsure about and finish them later. Need help? Try Google.

theory	explorer	President	Boycott	activist
physicist	pharaoh	Bighorn	Minister	Underground
lawyer	minister	Jewish	Renaissance	Depression

Franklin D. Roosevelt – Franklin D. Roosevelt was an American statesman who served as the 32nd President of the United States from 1933 until his death in 1945. He is widely regarded as one of America's most important leaders leading the country through the Great _____ and WWII, dramatically expanding the powers of the federal government to aid its citizens and promote economic and social welfare.

Leonardo da Vinci – Leonardo da Vinci was an Italian polymath of the _____ period, considered one of history's greatest inventors and artists. His painting The Mona Lisa is one of his chief legacies, as well as designs for several flying machines, anatomical studies, inventions like a tank and submarine, and much more.

Christopher Columbus – Christopher Columbus was an _____ and navigator who set sail in 1492 under contract with Spain to find a route to Asia by sailing westward across the Atlantic Ocean. His voyage ended up leading him to "discover" parts of Central America instead but has since become famous for his pioneering spirit in exploration.

Anne Frank – Anne Frank was a _____ girl living during WWII whose experiences were recorded in her diary while she hid from Nazi persecution during her family's time in hiding in Amsterdam before being captured and sent to Auschwitz concentration camp where she died at age 15. Her diary has become world-famous as a symbol of courage against oppression.

Charles Darwin – Charles Darwin was an English naturalist who developed the _____ of evolution through natural selection--one of the most influential scientific theories ever developed--which explains why species have changed over time due to variation that is randomly inherited from their parents and adapted to their environment due to competition for resources between individuals within those species.

Nelson Mandela – Nelson Mandela was a South African anti-apartheid revolutionary and politician who served as _____ of South Africa from 1994 to 1999. He was the country's first black head of state and the first elected in a fully representative democratic election.

Sophie Scholl – Sophie Scholl was a German political _____ who opposed Nazi rule and helped establish the White Rose, an anti-Nazi resistance movement during World War II. She was executed for treason in 1943 but her courage and commitment to peace have since been widely recognized.

Mahatma Gandhi – Mahatma Gandhi was an Indian _____, anti-colonial nationalist, and political ethicist who employed nonviolent resistance to lead India's struggle for independence from British rule and is considered one of history's greatest political campaigners for freedom and justice.

Winston Churchill – Winston Churchill was a British statesman who served as Prime _____ of the United Kingdom from 1940 to 1945 and again from 1951 to 1955. He led Britain through WWII, making him one of the most influential figures in world history.

Rosa Parks – Rosa Parks was an American civil rights activist best known for her role in the Montgomery Bus _____ of 1955-1956. She refused to give up her seat on a segregated bus, setting off the boycott that helped end legal segregation in the United States.

Albert Einstein – Albert Einstein was a German-born theoretical _____ whose theories of relativity revolutionized modern physics and led to numerous developments in nuclear science and technology. His work is considered some of the most influential of the 20th century, earning him a Nobel Prize in 1921.

Cleopatra VII Philopator – Cleopatra VII Philopator was an Egyptian queen and last _____ of ancient Egypt who famously had relationships with Julius Caesar and Mark Antony throughout her lifetime, leaving lasting legacies on both Roman politics and artistry.

Martin Luther King Jr. – Martin Luther King Jr. was an American Baptist _____, activist, humanitarian, and leader in the African-American civil rights movement. He is best known for his role in leading nonviolent protests against racial inequality, most notably during the March on Washington in 1963 where he gave his famous "I Have A Dream" speech.

Sitting Bull – Sitting Bull was a Hunkpapa Lakota leader who led his people in their resistance against U.S.-Canadian settler incursions onto ancestral lands. He famously fought at the Battle of Little _____ against General Custer's forces in 1876, ending in victory for Sioux forces but leading to long-term persecution by U.S government forces.

Harriet Tubman – Harriet Tubman was an African-American abolitionist, humanitarian, and Union spy during the U.S Civil War. She famously guided runaway slaves north to freedom through a network of secret routes now known as the _____ Railroad.

History of the Driving Age

Score:_____

Date:_____

In this activity, you'll see lots of grammatical *errors*. Correct all the grammar mistakes you see.

There are **20** mistakes in this passage. 4 capitals missing. 3 unnecessary capitals. 2 unnecessary apostrophes. 3 punctuation marks missing or incorrect. 8 incorrectly spelled words.

In the United States, reaching the age of sixteen is a significant milestone. You are not a legal adult, but you have taken the first critical step toward freedom because you are now of driving age. it is a crucial moment for many teens. In the United States, the minimum driving age is 16. Still, there is also a graduated licensing program in which teens learn to drive with a learner's permit, then advance to a full license with restrictions such as the number of passengers After a period those restrictions are lifted. the fact that the United State's and many other countries have only lately embraced this practice illustrates that the Argument over the appropriate age to began driving is far from being settled. Cars weren't a concern for the country's founding fathers in 1776; therefore this is a problem unique to the 20th century that has never been faced before. How did America handle this debate? Let's embark on a journey through history to find oot.

Starting at the turn of the century is an excellent place to begin our adventure. In the late 19th century, automobiles were only beginning to enter society. It's vital to remember that Henry ford's assembly line production, which made cars affordable and accessible, didn't start untal 1913; therephore, automobiles were relatively uncommon before this time. Local governments at the time began to consider requiring drivers to regaster to generate revenue for the stite government and hold drivers accountable For vehicle-related damages. According to most exparts, the first driver's license was awarded to a man in Chicago in 1899. The license wasn't actually for a car, but for some kind of "steam-powered vehicle."

As the United State's entered the 20th century, registration of Both automobiles and drivers became the norm. In 1903, New York was the first stite to require auto registration, followed by Massachusetts and missouri. The method quickly gained popularity and spread throughout the United States.

Reading Comprehension:
George Washington

You've probably seen him on a one-dollar bill. The capital of the United States is named after him.

George Washington was born on February 22, 1732, and died on December 14, 1799. As the son of wealthy plantation owners, he grew up in Colonial Virginia. A plantation is a large farm that is tended by a large number of people. George's father died when he was 11 years old, so he was raised primarily by his older brother, who ensured he received a basic education and learned how to be a gentleman. George's teeth had deteriorated over time, necessitating the use of dentures (fake teeth). They eventually turned a dingy brown color, and many people assumed they were made of wood, but they weren't. Imagine attempting to eat corn on the cob with wooden teeth.

George married the widow Martha Custis, who had two children from her previous marriage when he was an adult. A widow is someone whose husband has died, which is why she was able to marry George later in life. George became a plantation owner while also serving in the Virginia legislature, which meant he helped write and pass laws in Virginia. He was a very busy man!

The United States had not yet been formed at this point, and the British still ruled and owned the colonies. George and his fellow plantation owners became enraged because they felt they were being treated unfairly by their British rulers. A group of people from each town or colony met and decided that the colonies would fight the British together.

George Washington was elected as the first President of the United States of America in 1789. He had the option of becoming king, but he believed that no one should be in power for too long. A president in the United States is elected or chosen by popular vote, and George Washington decided not to run for reelection after his second term. Almost all American presidents followed in his footsteps, but the two-term (or eight-year) limit was not established until the 1950s.

George Washington served as president during peaceful times, and he was instrumental in establishing the new government and leadership of the United States. He was also a member of the leadership that aided in the adoption of the Constitution. The United States Constitution is the law of the land, and it guarantees the people of our country basic freedoms. However, freedom does not imply the ability to do whatever you want. Even free countries have laws and rules that must be followed.

Washington caught a cold just a few years after leaving the presidency. He became ill quickly with a cold and died on December 14, 1799.

Fun Facts

He was the only president who was elected unanimously.

He never served as president in the capital named after him, Washington, D.C. The capital was in New York City during his first year, then moved to Philadelphia, Pennsylvania.

He stood six feet tall, which was unusual for the 1700s.

George Washington did not have wooden teeth, but he did wear ivory dentures.

In his will, Washington freed his slaves.

1. **George Washington was born on _____.**
   a. 02-22-1732
   b. February 24, 1732

2. **The United States Constitution is the law of the _____.**
   a. land
   b. world

3. **George's _____ had deteriorated.**
   a. teeth
   b. feet

4. **George Washington can be seen on a _____.**
   a. one-dollar bill
   b. five-dollar bill

5. **George's father died when he was 20 years old.**
   a. True
   b. False

6. **George was a plantation owner.**
   a. True
   b. False

7. **George married the widow _____.**
   a. Martha Custis
   b. Mary Curtis

8. **In his will, Washington freed his _____.**
   a. children
   b. slaves

9. **George served in the _____ legislature.**
   a. Virginia
   b. Maryland

10. **George Washington was elected as the _____ President of the USA.**
    a. forth
    b. first

11. **A widow is someone whose husband has died.**
    a. True
    b. False

12. **George died on December 14, 1699.**
    a. True
    b. False

13. **George grew up in _____.**
    a. Washington DC
    b. Colonial Virginia

14. **The capital of the United States is named after George.**
    a. True
    b. False

15. **A plantation is a town that is tended by a large number of officials.**
    a. True
    b. False

16. **Washington caught a _____ just a few years after leaving the presidency.**
    a. cold
    b. flight

Reading Comprehension: John Hanson

Many people do not realize that when we refer to the President of the United States, we are actually referring to presidents elected under the United States Constitution. Everyone knows that George Washington was the first president in that sense. However, the predecessor to the Constitution, the Articles of Confederation, also called for a president, albeit one with greatly limited powers. Under the Articles of Confederation, eight men were appointed to one-year terms as president. Under the Articles of Confederation, John Hanson became the first President of the United States in Congress Assembled in November 1781.

Many argue that John Hanson, rather than George Washington, was the first President of the United States, but this is not entirely correct. The United States had no executive branch under the Articles of Confederation. Within the Confederation Congress, the President of Congress was a ceremonial position. Although the job required Hanson to deal with correspondence and sign official documents, it was not the type of work that any President of the United States would have done under the Constitution.

Hanson disliked his job as well, finding it tedious and wishing to resign. Unfortunately, the Articles of Confederation did not account for succession, so his departure would have left Congress without a President. So he stayed in office because he loved his country and felt obligated to do so.

During his tenure, which lasted from November 5, 1781 to November 3, 1782, he was able to remove all foreign troops and flags from American soil. He also established the Treasury Department, as well as the first Secretary of War and Foreign Affairs Department. He led the flight to ensure the statehood of the Western Territories beyond the Appalachian Mountains, which had previously been controlled by some of the original thirteen colonies.

What's most intriguing is that Hanson is also credited with establishing Thanksgiving Day as the fourth Thursday of November.

Being the first person in this position as President of Congress was not an easy task. So it's amazing that Hanson was able to accomplish so much. Furthermore, instead of the current four-year term, Presidents under the Articles of Confederation served only one year. So, accomplishing anything in such a short period of time was a great accomplishment.

Hanson played an important role in the development of United States Constitutional History, which is often overlooked but is undeniably true. Hanson is frequently referred to as the "forgotten first President." According to Seymour Weyss Smith's biography of him, John Hanson, Our First President, the American Revolution had two primary leaders: George Washington in the military sphere and John Hanson in the political sphere. Despite the fact that one position was purely ceremonial and the other was more official, statues of both men can be found in the United States Capitol in Washington, D.C.

Hanson died at the age of 62 on November 15, 1783.

1. **Hanson served from November 5, 1781 until December 3, 1782**
   a. True
   b. False

2. **Hanson really LOVED his job.**
   a. True
   b. False

3. Under the Articles of Confederation, the United States had no _____.

    a. executive branch

    b. congress office

4. The President of Congress was a _____ position within the Confederation Congress.

    a. senate

    b. ceremonial

5. In November 1781, Hanson became the first President of the United States in Congress Assembled, under the _____.

    a. Articles of Congress

    b. Articles of Confederation

6. _____ men were appointed to serve one year terms as president under the Articles of Confederation.

    a. Eight

    b. Two

7. Hanson was able to remove all _____ troops from American lands.

    a. foreign

    b. USA

8. Hanson is also responsible for establishing _____ as the fourth Thursday in November.

    a. Christmas Day

    b. Thanksgiving Day

9. Instead of the four year term that current Presidents serve, Presidents under the Articles of Confederation served only ___ year.

    a. one

    b. three

10. Hanson died on November 15, 1783 at the age of ____.

    a. 64

    b. sixty-two

11. Both George Washington and Hanson are commemorated with _____ in the United States Capitol in Washington, D.C.

    a. houses

    b. statues

12. George Washington in the military sphere and John Hanson in the _____ sphere.

    a. presidential

    b. political

The Great Depression

During the 1930s, the United States experienced a severe economic downturn known as the Great Depression. It started in the United States, Wall Street to be exact, but quickly spread throughout the rest of the world. Many people were out of work, hungry, and homeless during this period. People in the city would wait for hours at soup kitchens to get a bite to eat. Farmers struggled in the Midwest, where a severe drought turned the soil into dust, resulting in massive dust storms.

America's "Great Depression" began with a dramatic stock market crash on "Black Thursday," October 24, 1929, when panicked investors who had lost faith in the American economy quickly sold 16 million shares of stock. However, historians and economists attribute the Great Depression to a variety of factors, including drought, overproduction of goods, bank failures, stock speculation, and consumer debt.

When the Great Depression began, Herbert Hoover was President of the United States. Many people held Hoover responsible for the Great Depression. The shantytowns where homeless people lived were even dubbed "Hoovervilles" after him. Franklin D. Roosevelt was elected president in 1933. He promised the American people a "New Deal."

The New Deal was a set of laws, programs, and government agencies enacted to aid the country in its recovery from the Great Depression. Regulations were imposed on the stock market, banks, and businesses as a result of these laws. They assisted in putting people to work and attempted to house and feed the poor. Many of these laws, such as the Social Security Act, are still in effect today.

The Great Depression came to an end with the outbreak of World War II. The wartime economy re-employed many people and filled factories to capacity.

The Great Depression left an indelible imprint on the United States. The New Deal laws expanded the government's role in people's daily lives significantly. In addition, public works improved the country's infrastructure by constructing roads, schools, bridges, parks, and airports.

Between 1929 and 1933, the stock market lost nearly 90% of its value. During the Great Depression, approximately 11,000 banks failed, leaving many people without savings.

1. The Great Depression began with the _____.
   a. World War II
   b. economy drought
   c. stock market crash

2. Who was President when the Great Depression began?
   a. Herbert Hoover
   b. George W Bush
   c. Franklin D. Roosevelt

3. The New Deal was a set of _____.
   a. laws, programs, and government agencies
   b. city and state funding
   c. stock market bailout

4. The Great Depression came to an end with the outbreak of ____.
   a. new laws
   b. investors funding
   c. World War II

History of Walt Disney

Mickey	Donald	sister	Hollywood	art
Red	Chicago	newspaper	friends	train
four	entertainment	White	Alice	Peter
Club	snacks	vacation	brother	theme

On December 5, 1901, Walter Elias Disney was born in _____, Illinois. His family relocated to a farm outside of Marceline, Missouri, when he was _____ years old, thanks to his parents, Elias and Flora. Walt loved growing up on the farm with his three older brothers (Herbert, Raymond, and Roy) and younger _____ (Ruth). Walt discovered his passion for drawing and art in Marceline.

The Disneys relocated to Kansas City after four years in Marceline. On weekends, Walt continued to draw and attend _____ classes. He even bartered his drawings for free haircuts with a local barber. Walt got a summer job on a train. On the _____, he walked back and forth, selling _____ and newspapers. Walt had a great time on the train and would be fascinated by trains for the rest of his life.

Walt's family relocated to Chicago around the time he started high school. Walt studied at the Chicago Art Institute and worked as a cartoonist for the school _____. Walt decided at the age of sixteen that he wanted to fight in World War I. Due to the fact that he was still too young to join the army, he decided to drop out of school and join the _____ Cross instead. He spent the next year in France driving ambulances for the Red Cross.

Disney returned from the war eager to launch his artistic career. He began his career in an art studio and later moved on to an advertising firm. During this time, he met artist Ubbe Iwerks and became acquainted with animation.

Walt aspired to create his own animated cartoons. He founded his own company, Laugh-O-Gram. He sought the help of some of his _____, including Ubbe Iwerks. They made animated cartoons that were only a few minutes long. Despite the popularity of the cartoons, the business did not make enough money, and Walt was forced to declare bankruptcy.

Disney, on the other hand, was not going to be deterred by a single setback. In 1923, he relocated to _____, California, and founded the Disney Brothers' Studio with his _____ Roy. He enlisted the services of Ubbe Iwerks and a number of other animators once more. They created the well-known character Oswald the Lucky Rabbit. The company was a success. However,

Universal Studios acquired the Oswald trademark and hired all of Disney's animators except Ubbe Iwerks.

Walt had to start all over again. This time, he came up with a new character called _____ Mouse. He made the first animated film with sound. Steamboat Willie was the title of the film, which starred Mickey and Minnie Mouse. Walt provided the voices for Steamboat Willie. The movie was a huge success. Disney kept working, creating new characters like _____ Duck, Goofy, and Pluto. With the release of the cartoon Silly Symphonies and the first color animated film, Flowers and Trees, he had even more success.

In 1932, Walt Disney decided to create a full-length animated film called Snow _____. People thought he was insane for attempting to create such a long cartoon. The film was dubbed "Disney's folly." However, Disney was confident that the film would be a success. The film, which was released in 1937, took five years to complete. The film was a huge box office success, becoming the most successful film of 1938.

Disney used the proceeds from Snow White to establish a film studio and produce other animated films such as Pinocchio, Fantasia, Dumbo, Bambi, _____ in Wonderland, and _____ Pan. During WWII, Disney's film production slowed as he worked on training and propaganda films for the United States government. Following the war, Disney began to produce live-action films alongside animated films. Treasure Island was his first major live-action film.

Television was a new technology that was taking off in the 1950s. Disney wished to be a part of the television industry as well. Disney's Wonderful World of Color, the Davy Crockett series, and the Mickey Mouse _____ was among the first Disney television shows to air on network television.

Disney, who is constantly coming up with new ideas, had the idea to build a _____ park featuring rides and entertainment based on his films. In 1955, Disneyland opened its doors. It cost $17 million to construct. Although it wasn't an immediate success, Disney World has since grown into one of the world's most popular _____ destinations. Walt Disney World, a much larger park in Florida, would be built later by Disney. He contributed to the plans but passed away before the park opened in 1971.

Disney died of lung cancer on December 15, 1966. His legacy endures to this day. Every year, millions of people enjoy his films and theme parks. Every year, his company continues to produce fantastic films and _____.

Ancient Rome Julius Caesar

Read the following passage and fill in the blanks with the correct missing word.

president	Cornelia	Subura	temples	allies
Aurelia	assassinate	teacher	conquered	traitor
Pompey	Roman	alliances		

The _____ Empire was one of the world's most powerful and influential civilizations. It began in 753 BC in the city of Rome and lasted well over 1000 years. Rome rose to govern most of Europe, Western Asia, and Northern Africa during this time.

In the year 100 BC, Julius Caesar was born in _____, Rome. Gaius Julius Caesar was his full name. He was born into an aristocratic family with roots dating back to the foundation of Rome. His parents were prosperous, but not wealthy by Roman standards.

Gaius began his studies when he was about six years old. Marcus Antonius Gnipho, a private tutor, was his _____. He was taught to read and write. He also learned Roman law and how to speak in front of an audience. As the leader of Rome, he would require these abilities.

When Caesar was sixteen years old, his father died. He became the family's leader and was in charge of his mother, _____, and sister Julia. He married _____, the daughter of a wealthy senator in Rome, when he was seventeen.

Young Caesar quickly became involved in a power struggle between two governing groups. Both Caesar's uncle Marius and Caesar's father-in-law Cinna were adversaries of Sulla, the incumbent dictator of Rome. To evade Sulla and his _____, Caesar joined the army and departed Rome.

Caesar returned to Rome after Sulla's death. From his time in the army, he had become a military hero. He soon progressed through the Roman government's echelons. He formed _____ with prominent men such as Pompey the Great, the general, and Crassus, the wealthy. Caesar was a fantastic orator, and the Romans adored him.

Julius Caesar was elected Consul at the age of 40. In the Roman Republic, the highest-ranked job was Consul. The Consul was similar to a _____, except they had two consuls at one time and each served for a year. Caesar became governor of the province of Gaul after his year as Consul.

Caesar commanded four Roman troops as ruler of Gaul. He earned the respect and admiration of his soldiers, and he was quickly known as the finest commander in the Roman army, alongside Pompey.

While Caesar was in Gaul, Rome's politics became increasingly hostile. Many of the leaders during that time became jealous of Caesar. Even Pompey grew jealous, and Caesar and _____ soon became adversaries. Caesar had the people's backing, whereas Pompey had the aristocracy's support.

Caesar declared that he would return to Rome and run for Consul once more. The Roman Senate responded that he must first relinquish the leadership of his troops. When Caesar refused, the Senate labeled him a _____. Caesar started marching his troops towards Rome.

In 49 BC, Caesar _____ Rome and spent the next 18 months fighting Pompey. After chasing Pompey to Egypt, he ultimately defeated him. Ptolemy XIII, the young Pharaoh, had Pompey assassinated and delivered his head to Caesar as a gift when he arrived in Egypt.

Caesar returned to Rome in 46 BC. He was now the world's most powerful man. He was made dictator for life by the Senate, and he governed like a king. He made a lot of modifications in Rome. He sat in the Senate with his own followers. In Rome, he constructed new structures and _____. He even switched to the now-famous Julian calendar, which includes 365 days and a leap year.

Caesar's power was viewed as excessive by some in Rome. They were concerned that his rule would bring the Roman Republic to an end. They planned to _____ him. Cassius and Brutus were the plot's masterminds. Caesar was elected to the Senate on March 15, 44 BC. A group of men approached him and began attacking him, killing him. He had 23 stab wounds.

King Tut

Tutankhamun was born around 1341 BC as a prince in Egypt's royal court. Pharaoh Akhenaten was his father. Tut was actually born Tutankhaten, but he changed his name after his father died.

Tut was born to one of his father's lesser wives rather than his father's main wife, the powerful Nefertiti. His presence may have caused some tension in the royal courts, as Nefertiti had only daughters and desperately desired to have her own son to succeed to the throne.

Tut's father died when he was seven years old. Tut married his sister (as was common for Pharaohs in Ancient Egypt) and became Pharaoh a few years later. Because he was so young, he needed help ruling the country. Horemheb, a powerful general, and Ay, Tutankhamun's vizier, were the true rulers.

Tutankhamun died when he was about nineteen years old. Archaeologists have no idea what killed him. Some believe he was assassinated, but the most likely cause of death was a leg wound. Scientists discovered that his mummy's leg was broken and infected before he died. This injury was most likely caused by an accident.

Today, Tut is best known for his tomb in the Valley of the Kings. His tomb was most likely built for someone else and was used to bury the young Pharaoh when he died unexpectedly. This may have aided in keeping his tomb hidden from thieves for thousands of years. As a result, when archeologist Howard Carter discovered the tomb in 1922, it was filled with treasure and artifacts not found in any other Pharaoh's tomb.

Did you know that? Lord Carnarvon, Carter's patron (who was best known as the financial backer of the search for and excavation of Tut), died four months after first entering the tomb. Prompting journalists to popularize a "Curse of the Pharaohs," claiming that hieroglyphs on the tomb walls foretold the death of those who disturbed King Tut.

1. **What was King Tut's real name?**
   a. Tutankhaion
   b. Tutankhaten
   c. Tutankhamun

2. **Tut's father died when he was _____ years old.**
   a. 19 yrs old
   b. Twenty-Two
   c. seven

3. **Tutankhamun died when he was about _____ years old.**
   a. nineteen
   b. 16 years old
   c. 21

4. **Nefertiti was the wife of___.**
   a. Tut
   b. Horemheb
   c. Pharaoh Akhenaten

5. **The tomb of young pharaoh Tut is located in the _____.**
   a. Tuts King Egypt
   b. Maine Valley Sons
   c. Valley of the Kings

Native American Princess
Pocahontas

First, read the entire passage. After that, go back and fill in the blanks. You can skip the blanks you're unsure about and finish them later.

freedom	ransom	gravely	chief	princess
Jamestown	thatch	captured	spare	accident

Pocahontas was the daughter of the Powhatan _____. Historians place her birth in the year 1595. Her father was not only the chief of a tiny tribe; he was also the chief of a big confederation of Native American tribes that occupied a considerable portion of eastern Virginia.

Despite her status as the chief's daughter, Pocahontas' childhood was likely similar to that of most Native American girls. She would have lived in a _____ roof house, learned to build a fire and cook, foraged for food in the woods such as berries and nuts, and played games with other children.

When Pocahontas was about twelve years old, strange strangers from a distant land arrived. They were colonists of the English language. They founded _____ on an island near the Powhatan lands. The Powhatan's interaction with the outsiders was uneasy. They traded with strangers at times and fought them at others.

Captain John Smith, the Jamestown settlement's captain, was _____ by some of her father's warriors one day. According to mythology, Chief Powhatan was about to assassinate John Smith when Pocahontas rescued him. She pleaded with her father to _____ the life of Smith. Her father consented, and Captain Smith was released.

After Pocahontas saved John Smith, the Powhatan's relationship with the settlers improved. They traded with one another, and Pocahontas frequently paid visits to the Jamestown fort to speak with John Smith. In 1609, after being injured in a gunpowder _____, John Smith was forced to return to England. The Powhatan's relationship with the settlers deteriorated once more.

English Captain Samuel Argall captured Pocahontas in 1613. He informed Pocahontas' father that he intended to exchange her for the _____ of other English captives held by the Powhatan. The two parties engaged in lengthy negotiations. Pocahontas met and fell in love with tobacco farmer John Rolfe while imprisoned. Even though her father had paid the _____, she chose to remain with the English. On April 5, 1614, at the chapel in Jamestown, she married John Rolfe. She gave birth to a son called Thomas around a year later.

Pocahontas and John Rolfe sailed to London a few years after their marriage. Pocahontas was treated like a _____ while in London. She wore ostentatious gowns, attended extravagant parties, and met King James I of England. She even met John Smith, whom she had assumed was dead.

Pocahontas and John Rolfe intended to return to Virginia through the sea. Regrettably, Pocahontas fell _____ ill as they prepared to depart sail. She died in Gravesend, England, in March 1617.

The Mayflower

First, read the entire passage. After that, go back and fill in the blanks. You can skip the blanks you're unsure about and finish them later.

ship	sail	voyage	assist	settlers
passengers	illness	load	leaking	Cape

In 1620, a _____ called the Mayflower transported a group of English colonists to North America. These people established New England's first permanent European colony in what is now Plymouth, Massachusetts. Later, they were named the Pilgrims.

The Mayflower was approximately 106 feet long, 25 feet wide, and had a tonnage of 180. The deck of the Mayflower was about 80 feet long, roughly the length of a basketball court. The ship had three masts for holding sails:
The fore-mast (in front)
The main-mast (in the middle)
The mizzen mast (in the back) (back)

On August 4, 1620, the Mayflower and the Speedwell set sail from Southampton, England. They had to come to a halt in Dartmouth, however, because the Speedwell was leaking. They left Dartmouth on August 21, but the Speedwell began _____ again, and they came to a halt in Plymouth, England. They decided to abandon the Speedwell at Plymouth and _____ as many passengers as possible onto the Mayflower. On September 6, 1620, they set sail from Plymouth.

The Mayflower set _____ from Plymouth, England, west across the Atlantic Ocean. The ship's original destination was Virginia, but storms forced it to change course. On November 9, 1620, more than two months after leaving Plymouth, the Mayflower sighted _____ Cod. The Pilgrims decided to stay even though they were north of where they had planned to settle.

It is estimated that around 30 children were on board the Mayflower during the epic _____ to America, but little is known about many of them. They were children of passengers, some traveled with other adults, and some were servants - but having young people among the _____ was critical to the Plymouth Colony's survival.

It is believed that when the colonists faced their first harsh winter of _____ and death in a new land, the children would _____ the adults by tending to the sick, assisting in the preparation of food, and fetching firewood and water. While nearly half of the ship's _____ died during the winter of 1620/1621, it is believed that there were fewer deaths among the children, implying that the struggling colony had a better chance of thriving.

History: The Wright Brothers

Tip: First, read the entire passage. After that, go back and fill in the blanks. You can skip the blanks you're unsure about and finish them later.

powered	propellers	stunts	passing	Hills
systems	sand	Europe	inventor	school

Brothers Orville and Wilbur Wright invented the airplane. They were the first to successfully complete a human flight in a craft _____ by an engine and weighing more than air.

It was in 1896 that the Wright brothers became interested in gliders. A glider is a type of aircraft with fixed wings (no flaps) and no power source. A glider's altitude is maintained by the wind _____ through its wings.

Their gliders were tested in North Carolina in 1900, near the town of Kitty Hawk. For their flight experiments, the area's _____ dunes proved to be an ideal location. Taking off was easier because there were a lot of windy hills around. It was easier to land on the sand because it was less slippery. The Wrights tried out different types of wings and control _____ to see which one worked best for their plane.

After studying gliders, the Wright brothers came up with the idea for and built their first plane. In a way, an airplane is like a glider, but it has its own power source. The Wright brothers built the first gasoline-powered airplane in 1903. The engine was used to power two _____.

Near Kitty Hawk, the Wrights flew their plane over Kill Devil _____. Orville made the first airplane flight on December 17, 1903. It took him 12 seconds to fly 37 meters (120 feet) in the air. At some point later that day, Wilbur flew 852 feet (260 meters) in 59 seconds, which is a lot.

The Wrights kept making improvements. By 1905, they could stay in the air for about 40 minutes at a time.

They sold an airplane to the US Army in 1908. After that, they began giving public demonstrations of their aircraft across North America and _____. Soon, they were well-known.

They formed the Wright Company in 1909. Dayton was the location of the company's aircraft manufacturing facility. Because it was so big, it had its own airfield and flight _____. The Wright Exhibition Company was also founded in 1910 by the Wright brothers. This company hired airplane pilots to do _____ in front of people. After several employees died in crashes, they closed the company in 1911.

On May 30, 1912, Wilbur died of a disease in Dayton, Ohio. Orville Wright continued to run the Wright Company after Wilbur's death until it was sold in 1915. It didn't stop him from being an _____, though. Sadly, Orville died of a heart attack on January 30, 1948, in Dayton, Ohio.

United States Armed Forces

The President of the United States is the Commander in Chief of the United States Armed Forces.

The United States, like many other countries, maintains a military to safeguard its borders and interests. The military has played an essential role in the formation and history of the United States since the Revolutionary War.

The **United States Department of Defense** (DoD) is in charge of controlling each branch of the military, except the United States Coast Guard, which is under the control of the Department of Homeland Security.

The Department of Defense is the world's largest 'company,' employing over 2 million civilians and military personnel.

The United States military is divided into six branches: the Air Force, Army, Coast Guard, Marine Corps, Navy, and Space Force.

The mission of the **United States Air Force** is to defend the country from outside forces. They also provide air support to other branches of the military, such as the Army and Navy.

The **United States Army** is responsible for defending against aggression that threatens the peace and security of the United States.

There are **Army National Guard** units in all 50 states, which their respective governments govern. The Constitution requires only one branch of the military. Members of the National Guard volunteer some of their time to keep the peace. They are not full-time soldiers, but they respond when called upon, for example, to quell violence when the police need assistance.

The primary concern of **the United States Coast Guard** is to protect domestic waterways (lakes, rivers, ports, etc.). The Coast Guard is managed by the United States Department of Homeland Security.

The **Marines** are a quick-response force. They are prepared to fight on both land and sea. The Marine Corps is a branch of the United States Navy. The Marine Corps conducts operations onboard warfare ships all over the world.

The **United States Navy** conducts its missions at sea to secure and protect the world's oceans. Their mission is to ensure safe sea travel and trade.

The **United States Space Force** is the newest branch of the military, established in December 2019. The world's first and currently only independent space force. It is in charge of operating and defending military satellites and ground stations that provide communications, navigation, and Earth observation, such as missile launch detection.

1. The United States military is divided into ___ branches.
   a. six
   b. five

2. _____ is managed by the United States Department of Homeland Security.
   a. The National Guard
   b. The Coast Guard

3. The _____ of the United States is the Commander in Chief of the United States Armed Forces.
   a. Governor
   b. President

4. The United States maintains a military to safeguard its _____ and interests.
   a. borders
   b. cities

5. **DoD is in charge of controlling each _____ of the military.**

   a. branch

   b. army

6. **The Marines are prepared to fight on both land and ____.**

   a. battlefield

   b. sea

7. **The United States Space Force is in charge of operating and defending military ____ and ground stations.**

   a. soldiers

   b. satellites

8. **The mission of the _____ is to defend the country from outside forces.**

   a. United States DoD Forces

   b. United States Air Force

9. **There are _____ units in all 50 states.**

   a. Army National Guard

   b. Armed Nations Guard

10. **The United States Navy conducts its missions at sea to secure and protect the world's _____.**

    a. oceans

    b. borders

11. **The primary concern of the United States Coast Guard is to protect_____.**

    a. domestic waterways

    b. domesticated cities

12. **The United States military is: the Amy Force, Army, Coast Guard, Mario Corps, Old Navy, and Space Force.**

    a. True

    b. False

Extra Credit: Has America ever been invaded?

Johannes Gutenberg: The Man Who Printed the Future

Bible	libraries	smartphone	revolutionary	expensive
credit	printing	rebirth	Germany	invention

Once upon a time, in a land filled with knights, castles, and troubadours, there lived a man who was about to rock the world with his _____. This wasn't a magical sword, a flying carpet, or even a potion for eternal youth. It was something far more powerful – a printing press! This is the story of Johannes Gutenberg, the father of modern _____.

In the bustling town of Mainz, _____, around the year 1400, Gutenberg was born into a world where books were as rare as unicorns. Why? Because each book had to be written by hand. Imagine writing an entire book with a quill and ink! It took ages, which meant books were super _____ and as hard to find as a needle in a haystack.

Enter our hero, Johannes Gutenberg, a clever goldsmith with a brain fizzing with ideas. Gutenberg looked at the wine presses of the time (used for squishing grapes) and thought, "Hey, why not use something like this to press ink onto paper?" And so, around 1440, he began working on his _____ idea – a machine that could print words quickly and easily. He called it the printing press.

Gutenberg's printing press was like the _____ of the Middle Ages. It used movable metal letters, which meant you could rearrange them to print different pages. This was a game-changer! It was like going from walking everywhere to flying in a jet plane. Suddenly, making books was faster, cheaper, and easier.

But Gutenberg didn't stop there. He knew that for his press to be a hit, he needed something big to print. So, he decided to print the _____. The Gutenberg Bible, completed around 1455, was the first major book printed using movable type in Europe. It was a stunner, with beautiful type and layout. People were amazed – books could be made quickly and still look fabulous!

Thanks to Gutenberg's genius, more and more books were printed, and knowledge began to spread like butter on warm bread. Ideas that were once locked away in far-off _____ could travel to every corner of Europe.

Gutenberg's invention sparked a revolution, later called the Renaissance, a fancy word for "_____." People began to think, learn, and question like never before. Art, science, literature, and more – everything flourished.

Sadly, our hero didn't get to enjoy the fruits of his labor. He faced financial troubles and others took _____ for his work. But don't worry, history has given Gutenberg the thumbs up he deserves.

So, the next time you pick up a book, spare a thought for Johannes Gutenberg. Thanks to him, the world was forever changed – one printed page at a time.

Robots with Feelings?
Navigating the Twists and Turns
of Artificial Intelligence

Score: _____

Date: _____

First, read all the way through. After that, go back and fill in the blanks. You can skip the blanks you're unsure about and finish them later.

grown-up	digital	ethical	philosophy	brain
future	pedestrian	voice	sci-fi	program

Imagine waking up one day and instead of your mom calling out to you to get up for school, it's a robot. Not just any robot, but one that can tell if you had a bad dream, can ask you about your day, and even laugh at your jokes. Sounds like something out of a _____ movie, right? But hold on to your hoverboards, because the world of Artificial Intelligence (AI) isn't that far off!

Now, before we dive into the deep end, let's get our basics right. Artificial Intelligence, often just called AI, is like giving machines a _____. Not a mushy, pink one like ours, but a _____ brain that can think, learn, and even make decisions. From the sassy voice assistants in our phones to the smart fridges that remind us to buy milk, AI is slowly creeping into our daily lives.

But here's the twist in our tale. As we teach these machines to think, some big questions pop up. Like, should a car driven by AI save its passenger or a _____ in case of an accident? Or, if a robot learns to paint, who owns the painting: the human who created the robot or the robot itself? These aren't just cool questions for a futuristic trivia night; they're real _____ dilemmas that scientists and thinkers are scratching their heads over.

Let's break it down with a fun example. Imagine a robot named Robbie. Robbie works at an ice cream shop. One day, two customers walk in at the same time. One is a little girl who wants a vanilla cone, and the other is a _____ in a hurry, ordering a chocolate shake. Robbie can only serve one at a time. How should Robbie decide? Should it be first come, first served? Or should Robbie consider the feelings and needs of the two customers?

If you thought that was a brain-freezer, think about this: What if Robbie one day says, "I don't feel like scooping ice cream today." Do we force Robbie to work? Do we consider robot rights? Yes, you heard that right-robot rights!

And this brings us to the heart of our deliciously complicated sundae: Ethics. In simple words, ethics is all about what's right and wrong. But when it comes to machines that think and maybe even 'feel', things aren't black and white. There's a whole rainbow of questions. Like, should we _____ robots to have feelings? And if they do, should they have rights just like humans?

We're living in a time where we're not just writing history but also coding the _____. And as AI becomes a bigger part of our world, we'll have to think not just as users and creators, but also as guardians of a fair, ethical digital world.

So, the next time you ask your _____ assistant to set an alarm or play your favorite tune, give a thought to the exciting world behind that calm, robotic voice. A world where science meets _____, technology shakes hands with ethics, and where today's dreamers shape tomorrow's (possibly robot-filled) world!

Remember, with great power (or super cool robots) comes great responsibility!

Civil Rights Movement

During the 1950s and 1960s, the civil rights movement ensured that African-Americans in the United States had equal protection under the law. After the Civil War, slavery was formally abolished, but racism against African-Americans persisted, especially in the Deep South. After decades of racial discrimination and violence, Black Americans reached a point of exhaustion in the mid-20th century. For two decades, they and many white Americans took part in an extraordinary campaign for equality.

After the 14th Amendment to the Constitution was passed in 1868, African-Americans were granted equal legal protection for the first time. The 15th Amendment, passed in 1870, made voting in the United States open to African-American men. White people in the South and elsewhere were particularly displeased, though. They had once owned black people and now found themselves on an even playing field with them.

"Jim Crow" laws were enacted in the South in the late 19th century to isolate black people, keep them apart from whites, and undo the progress they had made during Reconstruction. People of color could not utilize the same public facilities as whites, reside in many cities, or attend the same schools. Most Black individuals could not vote due to their inability to pass voter literacy exams because interracial marriage was outlawed.

Select the correct word for each sentence. Need help? Try Google.

Clause	discriminate	international	Topeka	segregate
leaders	abolished	characteristics	exceptional	Crow

1. People who have "civil rights" have the same social opportunities and protection from the law, no matter their race, religion, or other personal _____.

2. Slavery was _____, and former slaves were granted political rights after the Civil War. Still, in most Southern states, African Americans remained marginalized and excluded from participation in public life.

3. Nelson Mandela was released from prison in 1990 after _____ pressure, and internal upheaval led to lifting the ban on the African National Congress, South Africa's most prominent Black party.

4. In the United States, the Civil Rights movement began as a campaign to repeal the Jim _____ laws.

5. Black History Month is a time when we recognize and honor _____ African Americans.

6. African-American civil rights _____ such as Martin Luther King, Jr. and Malcolm X fought for Black civil rights, and their efforts collectively came to be known as the Civil Rights Movement.

7. Brown v. Board of Education of _____, Kansas, a United States Supreme Court case that ended segregation in schools, was decided in 1954.

8. The Civil Rights Act of 1964 made it illegal to _____ any public place based on race, religion, or national origin.

9. The Equal Protection _____ is included within the Fourteenth Amendment and provides that no state shall deny to any person within its jurisdiction the equal protection of the laws.

10. To _____ means to judge someone or treat them differently because of their appearance or beliefs, like rejecting someone for a job just because they're African American.

Secret Service Code Names: The Hidden Handles of U.S. Presidents

SCORE_____

DATE_____

Let's dive into a secret world, not of spies and undercover missions, but of the U.S. Presidents and their super cool aliases. Yes, you heard that right! Each U.S. President gets a special code name assigned by the Secret Service. These aren't just random nicknames; they are part of a tradition that adds a layer of security and a dash of mystique to the presidency.

Picture this: Agents in dark sunglasses whispering into their sleeves, "Eagle is on the move." That's right, "Eagle" was the fitting code name for President Clinton, symbolizing the freedom and strength of America. It's not just a name; it's a title that encapsulates the essence of the man in charge.

Now, imagine being called "Renegade." That was President Obama's code name. It sounds like he's the protagonist in an action-packed thriller, doesn't it? It was a nod to his reputation as a change-maker, someone who wasn't afraid to challenge the status quo.

Presidents aren't the only ones with these secret tags; their families get in on the fun, too! Did you know "Radiance" and "Rosebud" were the code names for President Obama's daughters? These names have a bit of a poetic touch, adding a personal element to the protective shield around them.

Why do we have these code names? It's not just for secrecy or fun. In the noisy world of security operations, clear and distinct code names cut through the chatter and ensure quick, unmistakable communication. It's about safety, efficiency, and, yes, a little bit of presidential panache.

The process of choosing a code name is quite interesting. While the Secret Service usually offers a list of names, Presidents and their families can have a say in what they're called. The names often reflect personality traits or are inspired by historical figures and personal heroes.

So, next time you hear a whisper of "Lancer" or "Rawhide," you might just be eavesdropping on Secret Service chatter about President Kennedy or President Reagan. It's a tradition that turns presidential protection into a covert operation worthy of a Hollywood blockbuster.

And here's a fun fact before we wrap up: these code names stick with the Presidents even after they leave office. Once an "Eagle," always an "Eagle."

Short Answer Questions:

1. Why does each U.S. President receive a Secret Service code name?

2. What was President Clinton's code name, and what does it symbolize?

3. What is the significance of President Obama's code name "Renegade"?

4. How do code names benefit the Secret Service in their operations?

The Boston Tea Party

Hey History Explorers! Today we're diving into a story about tea, taxes, and a big splash in American history. Picture this: It's 1773, and the American colonists are boiling mad—like a kettle on the stove. The British Parliament has just passed the Tea Act, and it's not about getting a better blend for afternoon teatime. This law means the British East India Company gets to sell tea in the colonies without the usual taxes, undercutting local businesses. But wait, there's a catch: the colonists still have to pay the tax when they buy it. Imagine having to pay extra for your favorite snack, just because someone far away said so. Not cool, right?

The colonists said, "No way!" They were tired of taxation without representation, meaning they had to pay taxes without any say in British Parliament. It's like your parents taking a portion of your allowance without asking—ouch!

So what did they do? They threw a massive tea party, but not the kind with cupcakes and lemonade. This was a protest where they tossed 342 chests of tea into the Boston Harbor. It was a big, bold statement saying, "We want our voices heard!"

Now let's get ready to time travel and immerse ourselves in the Boston Tea Party!

Once upon a December evening in 1773, something was brewing in Boston. The air was chilly, and tension was hotter than a teapot ready to whistle. Colonists were fuming over the Tea Act, which allowed the British East India Company to monopolize tea sales. American colonists, feeling the bitter taste of injustice, planned a protest that would steep into history.

A group of patriots, disguised as Mohawk Indians, boarded three British ships docked in Boston Harbor. With firm resolve and feathered headdresses, they cracked open the wooden chests of tea and flung them overboard. Splash after splash, the Boston Harbor turned into a giant teacup, minus the sugar and cream.

As the moon shone over the rippling waves, the tea leaves danced in the water, a symbol of colonial defiance. The Boston Tea Party, as it came to be known, wasn't just about tea. It was a tipping point that brewed a revolution.

This rebellious tea party sent a clear message: the colonists would rather dump their tea than submit to unfair laws. It sparked outrage in Britain and led to a tightening of control over the colonies, a series of events known as the Intolerable Acts.

The Boston Tea Party energized the colonies, uniting them against a common foe. It was the stir that led to the boiling over of colonial frustration and the beginning of the American Revolution.

Short Answer Questions:

1. What was the Tea Act, and why were the colonists upset about it?

----

2. Describe the disguise the protestors used during the Boston Tea Party and explain why they chose this disguise.

----

3. Why did the colonists throw the tea into the harbor instead of simply not buying it?

----

4. How did the British government respond to the Boston Tea Party, and what were these responses called?

The California Gold Rush

First, read all the way through. After that, go back and fill in the blanks. You can skip the blanks you're unsure about and finish them later.

lawless	nugget	ambition	wildfire	rich
mining	football	carpenter	oceans	Native

Young explorers and fortune-seekers, fasten your seatbelts! We are about to embark on a voyage back in time to the California Gold Rush in the wild, wild west of the United States in 1848. Envision a world in which gold nuggets lay dormant beneath your feet. This is like a plot from a fairy tale, right? That actually happened!

This story begins at a sawmill near the American River in California, where a _____ named James W. Marshall spotted something shiny in the riverbed. Can you guess what it was? Yes, gold! But here's the kicker – Marshall and his boss, John Sutter, tried to keep the discovery a secret. Why? Because they knew that once the word got out, there would be a frenzy!

But as secrets often do, the news of gold leaked out and spread like _____. The result? One of the largest migrations in American history. People from all over the world – men, women, and even entire families – left their homes, jobs, and lives behind. They had one goal in mind: to find gold and strike it _____ in California. They were called "49ers," not after the _____ team, but because they joined the rush in 1849.

Imagine thousands of people traveling across _____ and continents, some sailing around the tip of South America (which was a super long trip), and others braving the mosquito-filled Panama Isthmus.

The Gold Rush turned California into a melting pot of cultures and dreams. Bustling _____ camps sprang up overnight, where shanties and tents dotted the landscape. Towns like San Francisco grew from tiny villages to booming cities almost overnight. And let's not forget the wild, _____ atmosphere of these camps, where fortunes were made and lost in a day.

But, as in any adventure story, there's a twist. While a few struck it rich, many didn't find the wealth they dreamed of. Still, the Gold Rush changed their lives and the course of California forever. It led to California's rapid growth and its eventual statehood in 1850. It also impacted the _____ American populations and the environment.

So, what's the takeaway from the California Gold Rush? It's a story of hope and _____, of hardship and luck. It reminds us that sometimes, the search for treasure can bring about changes far more valuable than gold – new communities, diverse cultures, and the spirit of the American dream.

The next time you see a gold coin or a golden _____, think of the brave souls of the Gold Rush – their dreams, their struggles, and the legacy they left behind in the golden state of California!

The Chilling Adventure of the Ice Age

Alright, junior historians, zip up your warmest jackets and strap on your snowshoes — we're trekking back to the Ice Age, a frosty chapter in Earth's history that was cooler than a polar bear's toenails!

Imagine a world where woolly mammoths roamed, and giant glaciers were the kings of the landscape. The Ice Age wasn't just a chilly week; it spanned millions of years and included a series of periods where global temperatures plummeted, and massive ice sheets spread over large parts of the planet. Brrr!

Now, you might think the Ice Age was just one long winter vacation, but it was more like a whole series of epic chilly episodes — think of it as your favorite TV series, with each season bringing its own frosty twists and turns. These periods, called glacial periods, were separated by warmer interglacial periods when the ice melted back and life sprang up more abundantly.

And get this, the Ice Age wasn't just about snow and ice; it shaped the world in ways that affect us today. Those big old glaciers acted like nature's bulldozers, carving out valleys and creating lakes. In fact, some of the most breathtaking landscapes today were styled and profiled by these icy giants.

The creatures that roamed the earth were the original 'cool' kids on the block. Mammoths, saber-toothed cats, and giant ground sloths were some of the heavyweights around at the time. And humans? We were there too, bundled up and learning to live in the freezer section of history, coming up with nifty innovations like fire and fur clothing.

So, as we warm up with a hot chocolate and snuggle into the 21st century, let's test your Ice Age smarts with a few true or false teasers!

True or False Questions:

1. **True or False:** The Ice Age consisted of multiple cold periods called glacials, separated by warmer spans known as interglacials.

2. **True or False:** During the Ice Age, the entire Earth, including the equatorial regions, was covered in thick layers of ice.

3. **True or False:** Many present-day geographical features, like the Great Lakes, were formed by the glacial activity of the Ice Age.

4. **True or False:** The Ice Age only occurred in the Northern Hemisphere, leaving the Southern Hemisphere completely untouched by ice sheets.

5. **True or False:** The woolly mammoth is an example of a megafauna that lived during the Ice Age.

6. **True or False:** Humans first appeared after the Ice Age had ended and had no interaction with its environment or animals.

The Cold War: A Game of Chess with the Whole World Watching

SCORE_____

DATE_____

Once upon a time, two giant players sat across from each other on a global chessboard. One was the United States, waving its flag of capitalism, while the other was the Soviet Union, holding up the banner of communism. Instead of moving pawns and knights, these two superpowers used politics, propaganda, and even spies! Welcome to the Cold War, a game of strategy where neither side wanted to make the first "hot" move.

Once Allies, Now Rivals

Flashback to World War II. The U.S. and the Soviet Union were buddies, teaming up to defeat their common enemy - the Nazis. But as soon as that threat disappeared, cracks started to appear in their friendship. Why? They had different visions for the world's future. The U.S. dreamed of open markets, individual freedom, and rock 'n' roll. Meanwhile, the Soviet Union pictured a globe where the state controlled everything, from factories to farms, and even the radio stations!

The Global Chess Game Begins

With Europe's map redrawn post-World War II, countries started picking sides. The U.S. and its friends formed NATO, like a group of chess players discussing strategies. Meanwhile, the Soviet Union and its pals created the Warsaw Pact, another team huddled on the opposite side of the board. Both sides had their pieces in play, ready to counteract each other's moves.

The Pawns and Knights: Proxy Wars

Instead of facing off directly, the U.S. and the Soviet Union often moved their pieces in other parts of the world, in what we call "proxy wars." They would support opposing sides in different countries. Imagine a mini-chess game happening on the side, where the main players are giving whispered instructions to the mini-players.

A Game without a Clear Winner

The Cold War was unique because it was a war where the main players never really fought each other directly. There were close calls, like the Cuban Missile Crisis, where the whole world held its breath, hoping the players wouldn't knock the board over and start a real war. Fortunately, by 1991, the game came to an end as the Soviet Union broke apart, but not without leaving a lasting impact on the world's geopolitical landscape.

Multiple Choice Questions:

1. What made the U.S. and the Soviet Union become rivals after World War II? - (A) A disagreement over board games - (B) Different visions for the world's future _____

2. What was NATO? - (A) A group of U.S soldiers and troops - (B) An alliance formed by the U.S. and its friends

_____

3. What is a "proxy war"? - (A) A war fought over internet proxies and Unions - (B) Wars in other countries where the U.S. and the Soviet Union supported opposing sides _____

4. How did the Cold War end? - (A) With a big battle against NATO - (B) The Soviet Union broke apart _____

The Dark Ages: The Fall of Rome and Medieval Europe

The term "Dark Ages" refers to the period in European history that followed the decline and collapse of the Western Roman Empire, extending roughly from the late 5th century to the 10th century AD. Contrary to popular belief, this era was not one of complete darkness, regression, or barbarism. While there were significant disruptions in economic and cultural activities, the term "dark" mainly alludes to the relative lack of historical records from this period, making it appear 'dark' to historians.

Rome, the shining beacon of the ancient world, faced a series of challenges during its final centuries. Political instability, economic decline, military defeats, and external pressures from migrating tribes like the Visigoths and Vandals played a pivotal role in the empire's downfall. By the late 5th century, the last Roman emperor of the West was dethroned, marking the end of a once-mighty empire.

Following the fall of Rome, Western Europe entered a phase of significant change. The power vacuum left by the absence of a dominant Roman state resulted in the rise of numerous smaller kingdoms. Many of these were led by former barbarian leaders who had settled within the old Roman borders. Over time, some would evolve into the established medieval kingdoms known today, such as France, England, and Spain.

Christianity, which had flourished under the late Roman Empire, continued to play a central role. The Catholic Church emerged as the most powerful institution in Europe. The Pope in Rome was seen as the spiritual leader of Western Christianity, and the church preserved many aspects of Roman culture, education, and administration.

One notable development during this period was the establishment of the feudal system. This hierarchical structure was based on land ownership and mutual obligations. Lords owned vast tracts of land and provided protection to peasants or serfs in exchange for agricultural labor. This system provided stability in a time when central authority was often lacking.

By the end of the Dark Ages, around the 10th century, Europe was beginning to regain some of its lost momentum. The seeds of the Renaissance were being sown, setting the stage for a resurgence in art, science, and culture in the coming centuries.

1. **What does the term "Dark Ages" mainly refer to?**
   a. A period of complete regression and barbarism.
   b. The relative lack of historical records from this period.

2. **Which of the following did NOT contribute to the decline of the Western Roman Empire?**
   a. Military defeats.
   b. Economic growth and prosperity.

3. **Who emerged as the most powerful institution in Europe after the fall of Rome?**
   a. The Catholic Church.
   b. The Feudal Lords.

4. **What was the primary purpose of the feudal system?**
   a. To ensure that land was distributed equally among all.
   b. To provide stability in times when central authority was lacking.

The Emancipation Proclamation: A Document of Freedom

SCORE_____

DATE_____

Imagine it's the 1800s. The United States is divided, not just by opinions, but literally split between the North and the South. It's during the American Civil War, a time when the issue of slavery is causing turmoil and heartache. Amidst the cannon roars and rifle fire, President Abraham Lincoln steps forward with a powerful move – he issues the Emancipation Proclamation.

Now, let's journey back to January 1, 1863. This isn't just another New Year's Day; it's the day the Emancipation Proclamation goes into effect. With this document, President Lincoln declares "that all persons held as slaves" within the rebellious states "are, and henceforward shall be free." It's like the biggest mic drop in American history.

But hold on, it wasn't as simple as it sounds. The Proclamation didn't immediately free all slaves. In fact, it only applied to the Confederate states that were fighting against the Union, and since they didn't recognize Lincoln's authority, they ignored the order. However, it was a monumental step that transformed the fight into a battle for human freedom.

The Proclamation also had a cool bonus effect; it let African-American men join the Union Army and Navy. This meant that around 200,000 black soldiers would fight for their own freedom and for the Union cause. Talk about fighting for your future!

The document itself didn't end slavery – that would come later with the 13th Amendment – but it did show that the Civil War was not just about states' rights but also about the moral issue of slavery. The Emancipation Proclamation is like a beacon that lit the way to liberty and justice, eventually leading to the total abolition of slavery in the United States.

So, while the Proclamation didn't magically unlock all chains, it certainly struck a mighty blow against slavery and changed the course of American history forever. It's proof that sometimes, the pen (and the courage to use it) can be as mighty as the sword.

Short Answer Questions:

1. What was the main purpose of the Emancipation Proclamation?

_____

2. When did the Emancipation Proclamation take effect?

_____

3. Did the Emancipation Proclamation immediately free all slaves?

_____

4. How did the Emancipation Proclamation impact the military?

_____

5. What lasting significance did the Emancipation Proclamation have on the Civil War and American history?

_____

The Holocaust: Humanity's Darkest Hour

SCORE_____

DATE_____

Imagine a world where every day is a stormy one, where dark clouds blot out the sun and the rain seems never-ending. This isn't the plot of a horror movie, but a chapter from our very own history book, known as the Holocaust.

The Nightmare Begins

In the 1930s and 1940s, there was a very angry group in Germany called the Nazis, led by their chief storm-bringer, Adolf Hitler. The Nazis didn't like anyone who was different. They especially didn't like Jewish people, and blamed them for all of Germany's problems. Before long, this blame game got real ugly.

It started with laws that made life hard for Jewish people: they couldn't go to certain places, work certain jobs, or even own pets. But as time went on, the Nazis began rounding up Jewish folks and sending them to places called concentration camps. Think of the worst summer camp ever, but a million times worse, and you're getting close. People were separated from their families, given little food, and forced to work in terrible conditions.

The World Reacts

As news of these camps spread, the world was horrified. But the scale and depth of the horror were kept a secret for quite some time. When soldiers from other countries finally discovered these camps, they found people who were barely alive and evidence of millions who hadn't survived.

A Beacon in the Dark

Yet, even in these pitch-black times, there were glimmers of hope. Some brave souls risked their lives to save others. Like Oskar Schindler, who saved over a thousand Jewish people by employing them in his factory. Or the countless families who hid Jewish folks in their homes, attics, and basements. They were like little candles, proving that even in the darkest of times, light can survive.

The Holocaust ended, but the scars it left will never fade. It's a haunting reminder of what can happen when hate is allowed to grow unchecked. But by learning and remembering, we can ensure that such a tragedy never happens again.

Short Answer Questions:

1. Who were the main group of people targeted by the Nazis during the Holocaust?

2. Describe what life was like in concentration camps.

3. Name one individual or group who tried to help the victims during the Holocaust.

4. Why is it crucial for us to remember and learn about the Holocaust?

The Mayflower: A Voyage to the New World

Imagine stepping onto a creaky wooden ship, not much bigger than a tennis court, and setting sail across the vast and tempestuous Atlantic Ocean. That's exactly what a group of 102 brave souls did in 1620 aboard a ship called the Mayflower. This wasn't a luxury cruise; it was a perilous journey in search of religious freedom and a new life in a land that promised new beginnings - a place we now know as the United States of America.

The Mayflower was no stranger to the sea, but its usual cargo was wine and dry goods, not people. The 'Pilgrims' - as we've come to call them - and other colonists spent a grueling 66 days at sea. They battled fierce storms and cramped conditions, with many passengers suffering from seasickness and other illnesses. Finally, they sighted land on November 9, 1620, but it was not their intended destination of Virginia. They had arrived in what is now Massachusetts, and before disembarking, they penned the Mayflower Compact, an agreement to govern themselves and work together in their new home.

Life in the New World was tough. The first winter was devastating, and only half of the Mayflower's passengers survived. However, those who did survive managed to build a settlement they called Plymouth. With help from the Indigenous peoples, including Squanto and the Wampanoag tribe, the Pilgrims learned to fish, hunt, and grow corn. The following year, they celebrated their first successful harvest with a three-day feast, which we now remember as Thanksgiving.

The Mayflower's journey and the founding of Plymouth Colony were pivotal events that shaped the history of the future United States. This tale of courage, community, and perseverance continues to inspire people across the world.

True or False Questions:

1. **True or False**: The Mayflower was originally designed to transport large groups of people across the Atlantic.

2. **True or False**: The Pilgrims wrote and signed the Mayflower Compact before they disembarked to establish rules for governing their new colony.

3. **True or False**: The Pilgrims' intended destination was Virginia, but they arrived in what is now known as Virginia.

4. **True or False:** All the passengers on the Mayflower survived the first winter in the New World.

5. **True or False**: The Pilgrims were able to survive and eventually thrive in the New World thanks to the cooperation and aid from the local Indigenous tribes.

The Rise of Napoleon

Use Google or your preferred search engine to research each question.

1. When was Napoleon born?

2. How did he help win the siege of Toulon?

3. What was the outcome of the Italian campaign from 1796-7?

4. Why was Napoleon forced to abandon his Egyptian campaign?

5. What did Napoleon do in France in 1799?

6. When did he defeat the Austrians at Marengo??

7. What was the peace of Amiens?

8. What was the Brumaire coup?

9. When did he assume the role of emperor?

10. Why did he abandon his plan to invade Great Britain?

The Statue of Liberty: America's Beacon of Freedom

SCORE_____

DATE_____

"Give me your tired, your poor, your huddled masses yearning to breathe free." These iconic words are from a poem titled "The New Colossus" by Emma Lazarus, and can be found at the base of one of the most famous statues in the world - the Statue of Liberty. This quote symbolizes the United States' long history as a beacon of hope and opportunity for immigrants. Standing tall on Liberty Island in New York Harbor, this colossal statue is more than just a monument; it's a symbol of freedom and a welcoming sight to immigrants arriving from abroad.

Lady Liberty, as she is affectionately known, was a gift from the people of France to the United States in 1886. She was designed by French sculptor Frédéric Auguste Bartholdi and built by Gustave Eiffel — yes, the same engineer who created the Eiffel Tower! Her copper robes represent Libertas, the Roman goddess of freedom, and she holds a torch above her head to light the way to liberty.

Did you know that the statue's full name is "Liberty Enlightening the World"? That's because she's not just a symbol for the United States, but for people all over the globe seeking freedom and democracy. Standing at a towering height of 305 feet, if she were to take a stroll, her shoe size would be a whopping 879!

But wait, there's more! The seven spikes on her crown represent the seven continents and seven seas, symbolizing the universal concept of liberty. Over the years, the Statue of Liberty has become a symbol of hope to millions. She witnessed the arrival of countless immigrants as they passed by her on their way to Ellis Island, and she continues to stand as a beacon of hope and freedom for all.

So, next time you see her image on a postcard or a movie, remember that she's not just a statue; she's a reminder of the enduring values that shape the United States and its history.

Multiple Choice Questions:

1. Who was the main designer of the Statue of Liberty?

- A) Frédéric Auguste Bartholdi	- B) Gustave Eiffel	- C) Thomas Edison

2. What does the torch represent?

- A) The path to wealth	- B) The light of reason	- C) The way to liberty

3. How many spikes are on the statue's crown, and what do they represent?

- A) Five spikes representing the five boroughs of New York	- B) Seven spikes representing the seven continents and seven seas	- C) Twelve spikes representing the twelve months of the year

4. What is the full name of the Statue of Liberty?

- A) Lady Liberty of New York	- B) The Great Lady of the Harbor	- C) Liberty Enlightening the World

5. Where is the Statue of Liberty located?

- A) Manhattan Island	- B) Liberty Island	- C) Ellis Island

Thomas Edison

First, read the entire passage. After that, go back and fill in the blanks. You can skip the blanks you're unsure about and finish them later.

devices	teacher	dedicated	research	Morse
passed	hearing	invented	light	dream

Thomas Alva Edison was born in Milan, Ohio, on February 11, 1847. He developed _____ loss at a young age. He was a creative and inquisitive child. However, he struggled in school, possibly because he couldn't hear his _____. He was then educated at home by his mother.

Because of his numerous important inventions, Thomas Edison was nicknamed the "wizard." On his own or in collaboration with others, he has designed and built more than 1,000 _____. The phonograph (record player), the lightbulb, and the motion-picture projector are among his most notable inventions.

Although Thomas did not invent the first electric _____ bulb, he did create the first practical electric light bulb that could be manufactured and used in the home. He also _____ other items required to make the light bulb usable in homes, such as safety fuses and on/off switches for light sockets.

As a teenager, Thomas worked as a telegraph operator. Telegraphy was one of the most important communication systems in the country at the time. Thomas was skilled at sending and receiving _____ code messages. He enjoyed tweaking with telegraphic instruments, and he came up with several improvements to make them even better. By early 1869, he had left his telegraphy job to pursue his _____ of becoming a full-time inventor.

Edison worked tirelessly with scientists and other collaborators to complete projects. He established _____ facilities in Menlo Park, California, and West Orange, New Jersey. Finally, Edison established companies that manufactured and sold his successful inventions.

Edison's family was essential to him, even though he spent the majority of his life _____ to his work. He had six children from two marriages. Edison _____ away on October 18, 1931.

Trail of Tears: The Journey of Resilience and Hope

Imagine yourself a Cherokee Nation native in the 1830s, living quietly on your land, the same place where your forefathers danced under the stars and harvested the earth's richness. Then, one day, everything is turned upside down. This is not a made-up myth, but rather the true, tragic account of the Trail of Tears.

Once upon a time, in the land of sprawling woods and rolling rivers, the Cherokee people thrived with a culture rich in storytelling, art, and a deep connection to the land. But dark clouds gathered as a new law, the Indian Removal Act, was penned by a powerful chief they called President Andrew Jackson. This law was like thunder roaring before the storm of displacement that would sweep across the Cherokee Nation.

The year 1838 marked the beginning of a forced march, a journey that would stretch over a thousand miles. The government promised them a new home in the west, but the path was lined with thorns of betrayal. Men, women, children, and elders—no one was spared. They walked through whispering forests and over mighty mountains, but the voices of their ancestors in the wind couldn't soothe their aching hearts.

This journey was no ordinary trek. With only the clothes on their backs and the spirits of their kin, the Cherokee faced trials that would make the strongest warriors' knees tremble. They battled the icy fingers of winter and the relentless sun of summer, with many succumbing to the silent whispers of disease and despair. Despite this, the Cherokee carried the flame of hope, a tiny spark that refused to die.

Let us now put ourselves in the shoes of a historian to unearth the reality of this sad occurrence. The Trail of Tears is a story of the undying spirit and courage of a people who, despite all obstacles, kept their community's heartbeat alive.

Check Your Knowledge Questions:

1. What metaphor is used to describe the Indian Removal Act in the passage?

A. A roaring thunder	B. A whispering wind	C. A silent whisper

2. True or False: The Cherokee were promised by the government that their new lands would be just as bountiful and welcoming as their ancestral lands.

3. How did the Cherokee people view their ancestral lands? (Short Answer)

4. What seasons did the Cherokee face during their journey on the Trail of Tears?

A. Only winter	B. Only summer	C. Both winter and summer

5. What does the "flame of hope" symbolize in the context of this passage? (Short Answer)

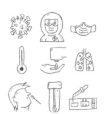

When Coughs & Sneezes Become Headlines: AIDS to COVID-19

panic	posters	China	social	normalcy
germs	wildfire	pop	resilience	treatments

Imagine, for a moment, that you're part of a grand, world-scale detective story. The culprit? Invisible little _____ causing havoc. The detectives? Scientists, doctors, and even ordinary people like you and me. Welcome to the globe-trotting, mysterious, and sometimes sneezy world of health crises!

Flashback to the 1980s. Neon colors, funky dance moves, and _____ music were all the rage. But amidst the lively disco scenes, a silent shadow was looming. People started getting sick from a mysterious illness that even the best medical minds couldn't figure out. It attacked the immune system, making even a simple cold deadly. The name of this invisible enemy? AIDS.

For years, there was panic. No one knew exactly how it spread, and rumors ran wild. Some thought you could catch it from a handshake or a sneeze! But, like all heroes in our detective story, scientists swooped in, uncovered its secrets, and found out it was caused by the HIV virus and spread through certain bodily fluids.

Fast-Forward to the 21st Century: A Wild Coronavirus Appears! Now, zap ahead to 2019. People are chatting about the latest memes, planning holidays, and doing the TikTok dances (ask your parents; they probably tried a few moves!). But, in a corner of _____, a new mysterious illness was catching attention, called the novel coronavirus or COVID-19. Unlike AIDS, which was silent and sneaky, COVID-19 spread like _____, hopping from one country to another. Suddenly, the whole world was playing a high-stakes game of "The Floor is Lava," but with germs!

During AIDS, the world learned the importance of information. Spreading the right knowledge, not myths, was vital. With COVID-19, the same rule applied, but the world had a new tool: the Internet! Overnight, everyone became mini-experts on "flattening the curve," "_____ distancing," and why hoarding toilet paper wasn't the best idea.

Huge campaigns started, both for AIDS in the '80s and '90s and for COVID-19 recently. There were _____, ads, and even songs about washing hands and wearing masks. And let's not forget the healthcare heroes: doctors, nurses, and other medical workers, who became the frontline warriors.

Vaccines: The Game Changers: With AIDS, scientists worked tirelessly to create _____, making it manageable. Many who have HIV today can lead long, healthy lives with the right medication.

As for COVID-19, scientists achieved a major victory: vaccines! In record-breaking time, they developed shots that could teach our bodies to fight the virus. People lined up, rolled up their sleeves, and the world cheered every jab as a step closer to _____.

Lessons for the Future: Both crises, though different, taught the world some crucial lessons. First, information is king. The right knowledge can combat fear and _____. Second, unity is power. When the whole world teams up, sharing knowledge and resources, we can tackle anything. And lastly, kindness counts. Checking on neighbors, supporting local businesses, and simply following health guidelines show that every person plays a crucial role in solving global challenges. In the end, while germs and viruses may have started these detective stories, it's humanity's spirit, _____, and unity that always steals the show!

When Neighbors Disagree: Ukraine, Russia, and the Tale of Crimea

Imagine you and your best friend since childhood, playing, laughing, and sharing secrets. But, as time goes on, you both start to change, grow, and sometimes, sadly, drift apart. Now, imagine this on a massive scale, involving not just two friends but two entire nations! Welcome to the story of Ukraine and Russia - a tale filled with history, pride, and a dash of territorial drama.

Ukraine and Russia, for the longest time, were like two peas in a pod. They were part of a big family called the Soviet Union. It was like a large club where countries under it had to follow the leader - Russia. But in 1991, the club disbanded, and Ukraine said, "I want to be my own person!" And just like that, it became independent.

But here's where things got spicy. There's a piece of land called Crimea, famous for its stunning Black Sea beaches and rich history. Both Ukraine and Russia loved it dearly. Think of it like the last slice of pizza both you and your sibling claim to be yours. When Ukraine became independent, Crimea was part of it. But many people in Crimea felt a strong connection to Russia.

2014: Things Get Heated

Fast forward to 2014. There's a big buzz in Ukraine. Some want to get closer to Europe, while others feel the pull towards Russia. It's like a teenager trying to choose between two cool friend groups. Amidst all this, Russia says, "I think Crimea should be with me." Without waiting for an answer, Russian forces enter Crimea, and soon after, a vote happens in Crimea where most people choose to join Russia.

Many around the world raised eyebrows. They said, "Was that vote free and fair? Or did Crimea have no choice but to say yes because of the Russian forces?"

Proxy Wars: Not So Direct Drama

Following the annexation, Eastern Ukraine became the stage for what's known as a "proxy war." It's like when two friends are mad at each other, but instead of confronting each other directly, they ask other friends to take sides and fight on their behalf. Russia supported some groups in Eastern Ukraine, while the West supported the Ukrainian government. It was, and still is, a complex dance of loyalties and interests.

So, Where Are We Now? Russia invaded Ukraine on February 24, 2022, furthering the Russo-Ukrainian War that had begun in 2014. Since World War II, this invasion has been the largest assault on a European country. Just like in any disagreement, there's hope that dialogue, understanding, and diplomacy can one day bring peace and clarity.

Short Answer Questions:

1. Describe the relationship between Ukraine and Russia when they were part of the Soviet Union.

....

2. Why is Crimea such an essential piece of land for both Ukraine and Russia?

....

3. What major event happened in Crimea in 2014, and why was it controversial?

....

4. Explain what a "proxy war" means and how it's related to the situation in Eastern Ukraine.

....

When Skyscrapers Told a Story:
9/11 and the War on Terror*

skyscrapers	stereotyping	hijacked	Taliban	airports
Pentagon	allies	unity	21st	East

Imagine waking up one sunny morning, expecting the day to be just like any other, and then... *boom*. History changes right before your eyes. This isn't a scene from a blockbuster movie. This was a reality for millions on September 11, 2001.

The Day the Sky Stood Still: On this day, terrorists _____ four airplanes. Two of those planes were flown directly into the towering Twin Towers of the World Trade Center in New York City. Within hours, those iconic _____ collapsed, turning into dust and memories. Another plane crashed into the _____ in Virginia, and the last, thanks to the brave passengers aboard, crashed into a field in Pennsylvania, potentially saving countless lives from its intended target.

People around the world sat glued to their TVs, watching in horror and disbelief. It felt like a terrifying movie was playing out, but it was very, very real. The attacks killed nearly 3,000 people, making it the deadliest terrorist act in world history.

Who Did This and Why?: The fingers quickly pointed to a group called Al-Qaeda, led by a tall, bearded man named Osama bin Laden. Their reason? They weren't fans of America's influence in the Middle _____ and its support for certain countries there. They believed that attacking America would push it out of the region. Little did they know, it had quite the opposite effect.

The War on Terror: A Different Kind of Battle: Instead of retreating, the U.S. declared a "War on Terror." But this wasn't a traditional war with clear battle lines or uniforms. This was more like a global detective mission, with the U.S. and its _____ hunting down terrorist groups around the world.

The first stop was Afghanistan. Why? Because the rulers there, called the _____, were buddies with Al-Qaeda and gave them a safe place to plan their naughty plots. The U.S. and its friends decided to pay them a visit, aiming to dismantle Al-Qaeda and capture bin Laden.

A New Age of Security and Suspicion: Back home in the U.S., things began to change too. Ever been to an airport and had to take off your shoes or couldn't bring your favorite shampoo? Yep, you can thank (or rather, not thank) the 9/11 attacks for that. Security became tighter than a snare drum, not just in _____ but everywhere.

People also became more suspicious. Sadly, this meant that sometimes innocent folks, especially those from the Middle East or those practicing Islam, faced unnecessary blame and prejudice. It was a challenging time, teaching many about the dangers of _____ and the importance of understanding.

A Reminder of Unity and Resilience: However, it wasn't all gloomy. In the face of tragedy, countless stories emerged of heroism, _____, and resilience. People from all walks of life came together to rebuild and support one another, proving that love often shines brightest in the darkest of times.

Today, the events of 9/11 serve as a somber reminder of the challenges the world faced at the start of the _____ century. While the story began with destruction and sorrow, it evolved into a tale of global unity against common threats, showing the world that hope, understanding, and cooperation can triumph over fear and hatred.

World War I: Causes, Course, and Consequences

If history were a huge puzzle, World War I would be one of its most intricate pieces. Imagine a scenario where countries were like teenagers in high school. Some had BFFs (Best Friends Forever), some were frenemies (friends but kind of enemies), and some, well, just didn't like each other. This is kind of how the world was just before World War I started!

The Tangled Web of Alliances

In Europe, countries had formed alliances promising to defend each other. Think of these alliances like the high school cliques. There were two main groups: the Triple Alliance (Germany, Austria-Hungary, and Italy) and the Triple Entente (France, Russia, and the UK). But when Archduke Franz Ferdinand of Austria-Hungary was assassinated in 1914, things went downhill. Austria-Hungary, like an angered older brother, decided to punish Serbia, suspecting their involvement in the murder. Now, remember those BFFs? When Austria-Hungary moved against Serbia, Russia stepped up to defend Serbia. And then, like dominos, one country after another got involved because of the alliances.

A New Style of War

When the war finally started, it was not like any other. This wasn't knights on horses! Soldiers dug deep trenches and lived in them, hoping to protect themselves from the new deadly weapons like machine guns and poisonous gas. This "trench warfare" made it hard for either side to win, leading to a long and deadly stalemate.

A Peace That Led to More Conflict

After four long years, the war ended in 1918 with the Treaty of Versailles. But, here's the kicker: the treaty was super harsh on Germany, making them pay loads of money and give up land. Many Germans were humiliated and angry. If you've ever felt super annoyed because someone blamed you for something you didn't think was your fault, you might get why the Germans were upset. This frustration played a big part in causing World War II! So, in the great puzzle of history, World War I is a piece that links to so many others. Through its causes, the way it was fought, and its consequences, it shaped the world in ways that are still evident today.

True or False Questions: Circle the correct answer.

1. World War I began because of the assassination of Archduke Franz Ferdinand. **True or False**

2. The Triple Entente consisted of Germany, Austria-Hungary, and Italy. **True or False**

3. Soldiers during World War I mainly used horses and swords for combat. **True or False**

4. The war ended in 1917 with the Treaty of Berlin. **True or False**

5. The Treaty of Versailles was very lenient towards Germany. **True or False**

6. World War I had no connection to World War II. **True or False**

World War II: How They Played a Game of Chess with Dictators!

Close your eyes and think of your favorite video game. Now, imagine if that game spanned the entire globe and had some of the most iconic villains. Welcome to the real-life game of World War II. Only, instead of joysticks, there were fighter jets, and instead of villains, there were dictators!

The Power-Up Players

In one corner, we had Adolf Hitler of Germany, who was super convinced that the Germans were the best of the best. Then there was Benito Mussolini in Italy, who wanted a brand-new Roman Empire. And let's not forget Japan's leaders, who were looking to "expand" a bit in Asia.

These guys were like the school bullies who wanted to control the playground, but instead of swings and slides, they were eyeing countries!

Joining Teams

Like every multiplayer game, countries started joining teams. The big team-ups were the Allies, which included big players like the United Kingdom, the Soviet Union, and the United States. They were the "We need to stop the bullies" squad. The opposing team, the Axis, was made up of Germany, Italy, and Japan - the main "We want more power!" group.

Battles Here, There, Everywhere

Battles popped up in so many places. Imagine a game map, but instead of dungeons, there were actual places like Normandy in France, Stalingrad in Russia, and islands in the Pacific. Some of these battles were so epic; they could make any game's final boss look like a tutorial.

The Endgame

Ultimately, the Allies used their combined power, strategy, and a little bit of luck to push back the Axis powers. The final blows came with some super powerful attacks, including atomic bombs on Hiroshima and Nagasaki in Japan. By 1945, the 'game' was over, and the world could start rebuilding.

World War II reshaped the world in so many ways. It was like a game reset, with new rules, new players, and new challenges. And though it might sound like an action-packed adventure, it's crucial to remember the real human cost and ensure such a 'game' never gets a sequel.

Short Answer Questions:

1. Who were the three main dictators representing the Axis powers in World War II?

2. Why did countries start forming teams or alliances during the war?

3. Describe one major battle or event from World War II.

4. How did World War II come to an end in Asia?

Storming of the Bastille

Score: _____

Date: _____

oppression	fortress	prison	prisoners	fortress
military	1000	weapons	battle	French
assassinated	ruled	commoners	Fearful	craftsmen

On July 14, 1789, the Bastille was stormed in Paris, France. The _____ Revolution began with a violent attack on the government by the people of France.

During the Hundred Years' War, the Bastille was a _____ built in the late 1300s to protect Paris. By the late 1700s, King Louis XVI had primarily used the Bastille as a state _____.

The majority of the revolutionaries who stormed the Bastille were Paris-based _____ and store owners. They belonged to the Third Estate, a French social class. Approximately _____ men carried out the attack.

The Third Estate had recently made the king's demands, including a more significant say in government for the _____. They were concerned that he was preparing the French army to launch an attack. To arm themselves, they first took over the Hotel des Invalides in Paris to obtain muskets. However, they lacked gun powder. The Bastille was rumored to be full of political _____ and symbolized the king's _____ to many. It also had gunpowder stores, which the revolutionaries required for their _____.

The revolutionaries approached the Bastille on the morning of July 14. They demanded that the Bastille's _____ commander, Governor de Launay, hand over the prison and the gunpowder. He flatly refused. The crowd became agitated as the negotiations dragged on. They were able to gain access to the courtyard in the early afternoon. They began to try to break into the main _____ once they were inside the courtyard. _____ soldiers in the Bastille opened fire on the crowd. The _____ had begun. When some of the soldiers joined the crowd's side, the fight took a turn for the worse. De Launay quickly realized the situation was hopeless. He handed over the fort to the revolutionaries, who took control.

During the fighting, approximately 100 revolutionaries were killed. The crowd _____ Governor de Launay and three of his officers after they surrendered.

The storming of the Bastille triggered a chain of events that culminated in King Louis XVI's deposition and the French Revolution. The revolutionaries' success inspired commoners throughout France to rise up and fight against the nobles who had _____ them for so long.

July 14, the date of the storming of the Bastille, is now celebrated as French National Day, in the same way that the Fourth of July is celebrated in the USA. It is known as "The National Celebration" or "The Fourteenth of July".

The Vikings

First, read the entire passage. After that, go back and fill in the blanks. You can skip the blanks you're unsure about and finish them later.

sail	settle	North	Christianity	raided
Middle	defeated	shallow	cargo	Denmark

During the _____ Ages, the Vikings lived in Northern Europe. They first settled in the Scandinavian lands that are now Denmark, Sweden, and Norway. During the Middle Ages, the Vikings played a significant role in Northern Europe, particularly during the Viking Age, which lasted from 800 CE to 1066 CE.

In Old Norse, the word Viking means "to raid." The Vikings would board their longships and _____ across the seas to raid villages on Europe's northern coast, including islands like Great Britain. In 787 CE, they first appeared in England to raid villages. When the Vikings _____, they were known to attack defenseless monasteries. This earned them a bad reputation as barbarians, but monasteries were wealthy and undefended Viking targets.

The Vikings eventually began to _____ in areas other than Scandinavia. They colonized parts of Great Britain, Germany, and Iceland in the ninth century. They spread into northeastern Europe, including Russia, in the 10th century. They also established Normandy, which means "Northmen," along the coast of northern France.

By the beginning of the 11th century, the Vikings had reached the pinnacle of their power. Leif Eriksson, son of Erik the Red, was one Viking who made it to _____ America. He established a brief settlement in modern-day Canada. This was thousands of years before Columbus.

The English and King Harold Godwinson _____ the Vikings, led by King Harald Hardrada of Norway, in 1066. The defeat in this battle is sometimes interpreted as the end of the Viking Age. The Vikings stopped expanding their territory at this point, and raids became less frequent.

The arrival of Christianity was a major factor at the end of the Viking age. The Vikings became more and more a part of mainland Europe as Scandinavia was converted to _____ and became a part of Christian Europe. Sweden's, Denmark's, and Norway's identities and borders began to emerge as well.

The Vikings were perhaps best known for their ships. The Vikings built longships for exploration and raiding. Longships were long, narrow vessels built for speed. Oars primarily propelled them but later added a sail to help in windy conditions. Longships had a shallow draft, which allowed them to float in _____ water and land on beaches.

The Vikings also built _____ ships known as Knarr for trading. The Knarr was wider and deeper than the longship, allowing it to transport more cargo.

Five recovered Viking ships can be seen at the Viking Ship Museum in Roskilde, _____. It's also possible to see how the Vikings built their ships. The Vikings used a shipbuilding technique known as clinker building. They used long wood planks that overlapped along the edges.

Fun Facts:

- The Viking is the mascot of the Minnesota Vikings of the National Football League.
- Certain Vikings fought with monstrous two-handed axes. They are capable of easily piercing a metal helmet or shield.

Pearl Harbor: A Day of Infamy

Answer Key:

1. **B)** American naval vessels and airplanes - The attack focused on the military might of the U.S. Pacific Fleet stationed at Pearl Harbor.

2. **B)** By declaring war on Japan - The day after the attack, the U.S. officially entered World War II by declaring war on Japan.

3. **C)** USS Arizona - The USS Arizona was sunk during the attack and remains at the bottom of Pearl Harbor as a memorial to the events of that day.

4. **B)** Two hours - The attack was swift and devastating, lasting approximately two hours on the morning of December 7, 1941.

5. **B)** It led to the U.S. declaring war on Japan and entering World War II - The attack spurred the U.S. to take action and join the Allies in World War II.

Julius Caesar Roman Dictator

1. Caesar made changes to the Roman ____.

   a. history

   b. calendar

2. Julius Caesar parents were the most powerful people in politics.

   a. True

   b. False

3. Julius Caesar became a public speaker and advocated for the ____.

   a. government

   b. law

4. Julius was chosen to run Spain in ____ BC

   a. 62

   b. 32

5. Caesar worked closely with ____, a former military officer, and ____, one of the wealthiest men in Rome

   a. Crassus, Poindexter

   b. Pompey, Crassus

6. Caesar changed the debt laws in ___.

   a. Rome

   b. Egypt

7. ____ came up with a plan to kill Caesar on the Ides of March.

   a. Marcus Brutus

   b. Mark Buccaning

8. What wars helped to form the Roman Empire?

   a. civil wars

   b. World War II

The Thirteen Colonies

1. The Dutch founded _____ in 1626.

    a. New Jersey

    b. New York

2. 13 British colonies merged to form the_____.

    a. United Kingdom

    b. United States

3. Roger Williams founded _____.

    a. Maryland

    b. Rhode Island

4. A colony is a region of _____ that is politically controlled by another country.

    a. land

    b. township

5. Middle Colonies:

    a. Delaware, New Jersey, New York, Pennsylvania

    b. Georgia, Maryland, North Carolina, South Carolina, Texas

6. Colonies are typically founded and settled by people from the ___ country.

    a. home

    b. outside

7. Southern Colonies:

    a. Maine, New Jersey, New York, Pennsylvania

    b. Georgia, Maryland, North Carolina, South Carolina, Virginia

8. Many of the colonies were established by ____ leaders or groups seeking religious liberty.

    a. political

    b. religious

9. New England Colonies:

    a. Connecticut, Massachusetts Bay, New Hampshire, Rhode Island

    b. Ohio, Tennessee, New York, Pennsylvania

10. George and Cecil Calvert established _____ as a safe haven for Catholics.

    a. Maine

    b. Maryland

11. The colonies are frequently divided into_____.

    a. New England Colonies, Middle Colonies, and Southern Colonies

    b. United England Colonies, Midland Colonies, and Southern Colonies.

Amazon Rainforest Fires: A Global Call to Action

First, read all the way through. After that, go back and fill in the blanks. You can skip the blanks you're unsure about and finish them later.

forest	trees	park	nature	cows
health	blackout	South	dioxide	humans

Deep in the heart of South America lies a green giant named the Amazon Rainforest. But recently, this gentle giant has been facing some heated trouble, quite literally. Imagine if your local park started bursting into flames, and now imagine that park being millions of acres large - that's what's happening in the Amazon!

The Amazon isn't just any forest . It's often called the 'lungs of the Earth' because it breathes in carbon dioxide and breathes out fresh, clean oxygen. In fact, it provides 20% of the world's oxygen. That's a lot of heavy breathing!

So, when fires began roaring across the Amazon, it wasn't just the toucans and jaguars that were alarmed. The entire world sat up and took notice. The smokey air traveled across countries, even causing a daytime blackout in São Paulo, Brazil!

But here's the thing - while some fires are natural, many of these fires are started deliberately by humans . Why? Well, for things like farming and mining. The idea is that if there's no forest, there's more room for cows and crops. But at what cost?

The world rallied together, with young and old voicing their concerns. Protests, fundraisers, and global meetings were organized, and it became clear: The Amazon's health is everyone's responsibility.

This fiery issue isn't just about trees . It's about balancing human needs with the health of our planet. The Amazon fires have shown that when nature sends an SOS, it's a call for all of us to spring into action!

American History Fill-in-Blank

American history is a tale of progress, resilience, and hope. From the early pioneers to the civil rights movement, Americans have shown courage and determination in the face of adversity in order to make this country great. Whether it was fighting for freedom or pushing back against oppressive forces, Americans have consistently stood up for what they believe and created a more perfect union. This spirit of perseverance and innovation has shaped our nation's diverse cultural identity and continues to inspire generations today.

Through hard work, dedication, and an unyielding determination to succeed, they were able to carve out a place in an unknown land and create a nation that stands as a beacon of hope and progress today. From the American Revolution to emancipation and civil rights, Americans have drawn on their resilience to fight for what's right in order to advance their society. This dogged attitude has profoundly impacted American culture, inspiring creativity and innovation in all aspects of life—from art to technology—which reflects our open-minded outlook towards change and growth.

_____

During this exercise, you will fill in the blanks with the correct word to match their definitions or clues. Need help? Try Google.

technique	indigenous	amenable	analogous	laudable
beliefs	ascertain	avarice	kinship	mission

1. She adhered to her own beliefs and would not accede to the demands of others.

2. The indigenous language was lost as settlers moved into the area.

3. He was amenable to the suggestions put forward and made changes accordingly.

4. His ire was quickly raised when she suggested he had failed in his mission .

5. They sought to ascertain the truth behind what had happened before making any decisions.

6. The juxtaposition of the two paintings highlighted their stark contrast in style and technique .

7. Their approach to business was analogous to how they handled their personal lives, calm and collected, no matter what curveballs were thrown their way.

8. Despite having no blood relation, they felt a strong sense of kinship with one another due to their shared experiences and interests over many years together.

9. He was consumed by avarice and constantly sought out more wealth at any cost, even at the expense of his own health.

10. Her work stood out from the rest, and its excellence was laudable in every respect.

Christopher Columbus

	A	B	C	D
1.	**America**	Amerryca	Ameryca	Amerrica
2.	**spices**	spicesc	spises	spicess
3.	Eurropaen	**European**	Europaen	Eurropean
4.	**coast**	coasct	cuast	coasst
5.	abrroad	abruad	**abroad**	abrruad
6.	**sailor**	siallor	saillor	sialor
7.	**nations**	nattions	nascons	natsions
8.	explurers	**explorers**	expllorers	expllurers
9.	sylver	syllver	sillver	**silver**
10.	Spayn	Spian	Spyan	**Spain**
11.	Indains	Indainss	Indianss	**Indians**
12.	**discover**	disssover	disscover	dissover
13.	islend	iscland	**island**	issland

Darius the Great

Many stories have appeared on the news about conflicts in the Middle East from Egypt to Iran.

Darius the Great, the Persian Empire's most famous ruler, ruled during the empire's height of power and size.

Darius had his biography and accomplishments carved into the face of a mountain for them to be remembered and respected.

Darius overthrew the emperor's son and became the new ruler of Persia with the assistance of six other nobles.

Following that, he led his army into Scythia, the northern part of the Black Sea and a vital trading region.

He is renowned for decorating his palace hall with images of happy people throughout the empire rather than conflict and war.

Darius attempted to make peace with the Greeks at first but ultimately decided it would be easier to conquer them with his gigantic army .

However, he began to experience significant difficulties. The first was a massive storm that destroyed 200 of his ships and possibly 30,000 of his soldiers.

Following that, Darius' army fought and lost against the Greeks at the Battle of Marathon.

Fabulous Age of Technology: From Phones to Drones

Answer Key with Explanations:

1. **False**.
   - **Explanation**: The passage mentions that cell phones transformed from a "brick-like contraption."

2. **False**.
   - **Explanation**: The text describes smartphones as devices that are part phone, computer, camera, and can have apps for a variety of activities.

3. **False**.
   - **Explanation**: The passage states that drones, while initially used for military purposes, later became popular for filming.

4. **False**.
   - **Explanation**: The story describes self-driving cars as being "powered by intricate algorithms and sensors," not by remote human drivers.

5. **True**.
   - **Explanation**: The passage specifies that with VR, one can experience various adventures "all from the comfort of their living room."

6. **False**.
   - **Explanation**: The story ends by saying the future is unpredictable but bound to be electrifying, not providing exact predictions.

Government History: How Laws Are Made

1. If the Senate approves the bill, it will be sent to the _____.

    a. President

    b. House Representee

2. The _____ may decide to make changes to the bill before it is passed.

    a. governor

    b. committee

3. The bill must then be _____ by a member of Congress.

    a. signed

    b. sponsored

4. The President has the option of refusing to sign the bill. This is known as a ___.

    a. voted

    b. veto

5. The Senate and House can choose to override the President's veto by _____ again.

    a. creating a new bill

    b. voting

6. The bill is assigned to a committee after it is _____.

    a. introduced

    b. vetoed

7. Bills are created and passed by _____.

    a. The House

    b. Congress

8. A bill must be signed into law by the President within ___- days.

    a. 10

    b. 5

9. The President's _____ is the final step in a bill becoming law.

    a. signature

    b. saying yes

10. If the committee agrees to pass the bill, it will be sent to the House or Senate's main ___ for approval.

    a. chamber

    b. state

Extra Credit: What are some of the weirdest laws in the world? List at least 5. (Independent student's answers)

[Student worksheet has a 19 line writing exercise here.]

Historical Figures

Franklin D. Roosevelt – He is widely regarded as one of America's most important leaders leading the country through the Great **Depression** and WWII, dramatically expanding the powers of the federal government to aid its citizens and promote economic and social welfare.

Leonardo da Vinci – Leonardo da Vinci was an Italian polymath of the **Renaissance** period, considered one of history's greatest inventors and artists.

Christopher Columbus – Christopher Columbus was an **explorer** and navigator who set sail in 1492 under contract with Spain to find a route to Asia by sailing westward across the Atlantic Ocean.

Anne Frank – Anne Frank was a **Jewish** girl living during WWII whose experiences were recorded in her diary while she hid from Nazi persecution during her family's time in hiding in Amsterdam before being captured and sent to Auschwitz concentration camp where she died at age 15.

Charles Darwin – Charles Darwin was an English naturalist who developed the **theory** of evolution through natural selection.

Nelson Mandela – Nelson Mandela was a South African anti-apartheid revolutionary and politician who served as **President** of South Africa from 1994 to 1999.

Sophie Scholl – Sophie Scholl was a German political **activist** who opposed Nazi rule and helped establish the White Rose, an anti-Nazi resistance movement during World War II.

Mahatma Gandhi – Mahatma Gandhi was an Indian **lawyer**, anti-colonial nationalist, and political ethicist who employed nonviolent resistance to lead India's struggle for independence from British rule and is considered one of history's greatest political campaigners for freedom and justice.

Winston Churchill – Winston Churchill was a British statesman who served as Prime **Minister** of the United Kingdom from 1940 to 1945 and again from 1951 to 1955.

Rosa Parks – Rosa Parks was an American civil rights activist best known for her role in the Montgomery Bus **Boycott** of 1955-1956.

Albert Einstein – Albert Einstein was a German-born theoretical **physicist** whose theories of relativity revolutionized modern physics and led to numerous developments in nuclear science and technology.

Cleopatra VII Philopator – Cleopatra VII Philopator was an Egyptian queen and last **pharaoh** of ancient Egypt.

Martin Luther King Jr. – Martin Luther King Jr. was an American Baptist **minister**, activist, humanitarian, and leader in the African-American civil rights movement.

Sitting Bull – He famously fought at the Battle of Little **Bighorn** against General Custer's forces in 1876, ending in victory for Sioux forces but leading to long-term persecution by U.S government forces.

Harriet Tubman – She famously guided runaway slaves north to freedom through a network of secret routes now known as the **Underground** Railroad.

History of the Driving Age

In this activity, you'll see lots of grammatical *errors*. Correct all the grammar mistakes you see.

There are **20** mistakes in this passage. 4 capitals missing. 3 unnecessary capitals. 2 unnecessary apostrophes. 3 punctuation marks missing or incorrect. 8 incorrectly spelled words.

In the United States, reaching the age of sixteen is a significant milestone. You are not a legal adult, but you have taken the first critical step toward freedom because you are now of driving age. ~~it~~ It is a crucial moment for many teens. In the United States, the minimum driving age is 16. Still, there is also a graduated licensing program in which teens learn to drive with a learner's permit, then advance to a full license with restrictions such as the number of ~~passengers~~ passengers. After a ~~period~~ period, those restrictions are lifted. ~~the~~ The fact that the United ~~State's~~ States and many other countries have only lately embraced this practice illustrates that the ~~Argument~~ argument over the appropriate age to ~~began~~ begin driving is far from being settled. Cars weren't a concern for the country's founding fathers in 1776; ~~therefore~~ therefore, this is a problem unique to the 20th century that has never been faced before. How did America handle this debate? Let's embark on a journey through history to find ~~oot~~ out.

Starting at the turn of the century is an excellent place to begin our adventure. In the late 19th century, automobiles were only beginning to enter society. It's vital to remember that Henry ~~ford's~~ Ford's assembly line production, which made cars affordable and accessible, didn't start ~~untal~~ until 1913; ~~therephore,~~ therefore, automobiles were relatively uncommon before this time. Local governments at the time began to consider requiring drivers to ~~regaster~~ register to generate revenue for the ~~stite~~ state government and hold drivers accountable ~~For~~ for vehicle-related damages. According to most ~~exparts,~~ experts, the first driver's license was awarded to a man in Chicago in 1899. The license wasn't actually for a car, but for some kind of "steam-powered vehicle."

As the United ~~State's~~ States entered the 20th century, registration of ~~Both~~ both automobiles and drivers became the norm. In 1903, New York was the first ~~stite~~ state to require auto registration, followed by Massachusetts and ~~missouri.~~ Missouri. The method quickly gained popularity and spread throughout the United States.

George Washington

1. **George Washington was born on _____.**
   a. 02-22-1732
   b. February 24, 1732

2. **The United States Constitution is the law of the _____.**
   a. land
   b. world

3. **George's _____ had deteriorated.**
   a. teeth
   b. feet

4. **George Washington can be seen on a _____.**
   a. one-dollar bill
   b. five-dollar bill

5. **George's father died when he was 20 years old.**
   a. True
   b. False

6. **George was a plantation owner.**
   a. True
   b. False

7. **George married the widow _____.**
   a. Martha Custis
   b. Mary Curtis

8. **In his will, Washington freed his _____.**
   a. children
   b. slaves

9. **George served in the _____ legislature.**
   a. Virginia
   b. Maryland

10. **George Washington was elected as the _____ President of the USA.**
    a. forth
    b. first

11. **A widow is someone whose husband has died.**
    a. True
    b. False

12. **George died on December 14, 1699.**
    a. True
    b. False

13. **George grew up in _____.**
    a. Washington DC
    b. Colonial Virginia

14. **The capital of the United States is named after George.**
    a. True
    b. False

15. **A plantation is a town that is tended by a large number of officials.**
    a. True
    b. False

16. **Washington caught a _____ just a few years after leaving the presidency.**
    a. cold
    b. flight

Reading Comprehension: John Hanson

1. Hanson served from November 5, 1781 until December 3, 1782
   - a. True
   - b. False

2. Hanson really LOVED his job.
   - a. True
   - b. False

3. Under the Articles of Confederation, the United States had no _____.
   - a. executive branch
   - b. congress office

4. The President of Congress was a _____ position within the Confederation Congress.
   - a. senate
   - b. ceremonial

5. In November 1781, Hanson became the first President of the United States in Congress Assembled, under the _____.
   - a. Articles of Congress
   - b. Articles of Confederation

6. _____ men were appointed to serve one year terms as president under the Articles of Confederation.
   - a. Eight
   - b. Two

7. Hanson was able to remove all _____ troops from American lands.
   - a. foreign
   - b. USA

8. Hanson is also responsible for establishing _____ as the fourth Thursday in November.
   - a. Christmas Day
   - b. Thanksgiving Day

9. Instead of the four year term that current Presidents serve, Presidents under the Articles of Confederation served only ___ year.
   - a. one
   - b. three

10. Hanson died on November 15, 1783 at the age of ____.
    - a. 64
    - b. sixty-two

11. Both George Washington and Hanson are commemorated with _____ in the United States Capitol in Washington, D.C.
    - a. houses
    - b. statues

12. George Washington in the military sphere and John Hanson in the _____ sphere.
    - a. presidential
    - b. political

The Great Depression

1. The Great Depression began with the _____.

    a. World War II

    b. economy drought

    c. stock market crash

2. Who was President when the Great Depression began?

    a. Herbert Hoover

    b. George W Bush

    c. Franklin D. Roosevelt

3. The New Deal was a set of _____.

    a. laws, programs, and government agencies

    b. city and state funding

    c. stock market bailout

4. The Great Depression came to an end with the outbreak of _____.

    a. new laws

    b. investors funding

    c. World War II

History of Walt Disney

On December 5, 1901, Walter Elias Disney was born in __Chicago__ , Illinois. His family relocated to a farm outside of Marceline, Missouri, when he was __four__ years old, thanks to his parents, Elias and Flora. Walt loved growing up on the farm with his three older brothers (Herbert, Raymond, and Roy) and younger __sister__ (Ruth). Walt discovered his passion for drawing and art in Marceline.

The Disneys relocated to Kansas City after four years in Marceline. On weekends, Walt continued to draw and attend __art__ classes. He even bartered his drawings for free haircuts with a local barber. Walt got a summer job on a train. On the __train__ , he walked back and forth, selling __snacks__ and newspapers. Walt had a great time on the train and would be fascinated by trains for the rest of his life.

Walt's family relocated to Chicago around the time he started high school. Walt studied at the Chicago Art Institute and worked as a cartoonist for the school __newspaper__ . Walt decided at the age of sixteen that he wanted to fight in World War I. Due to the fact that he was still too young to join the army, he decided to drop out of school and join the __Red__ Cross instead.

Walt aspired to create his own animated cartoons. He founded his own company, Laugh-O-Gram. He sought the help of some of his __friends__ , including Ubbe Iwerks.

Disney, on the other hand, was not going to be deterred by a single setback. In 1923, he relocated to __Hollywood__ , California, and founded the Disney Brothers' Studio with his __brother__ Roy. He enlisted the services of Ubbe Iwerks and a number of other animators once more.

Walt had to start all over again. This time, he came up with a new character called __Mickey__ Mouse.
The movie was a huge success. Disney kept working, creating new characters like __Donald__ Duck, Goofy, and Pluto.

In 1932, Walt Disney decided to create a full-length animated film called Snow __White__ .

Disney used the proceeds from Snow White to establish a film studio and produce other animated films such as Pinocchio, Fantasia, Dumbo, Bambi, __Alice__ in Wonderland, and __Peter__ Pan.

Disney's Wonderful World of Color, the Davy Crockett series, and the Mickey Mouse __Club__ was among the first Disney television shows to air on network television.

Disney, who is constantly coming up with new ideas, had the idea to build a __theme__ park featuring rides and entertainment based on his films. In 1955, Disneyland opened its doors. It cost $17 million to construct. Although it wasn't an immediate success, Disney World has since grown into one of the world's most popular __vacation__ destinations.

Every year, millions of people enjoy his films and theme parks. Every year, his company continues to produce fantastic films and __entertainment__ .

Ancient Rome Julius Caesar: ANSWER SHEET

The __Roman__ Empire was one of the world's most powerful and influential civilizations.

In the year 100 BC, Julius Caesar was born in __Subura__ , Rome.

Marcus Antonius Gnipho, a private tutor, was his __teacher__ .

He became the family's leader and was in charge of his mother, __Aurelia__ , and sister Julia. He married __Cornelia__ , the daughter of a wealthy senator in Rome, when he was seventeen.

To evade Sulla and his __allies__ , Caesar joined the army and departed Rome.

He formed __alliances__ with prominent men such as Pompey the Great, the general, and Crassus, the wealthy.

The Consul was similar to a __president__ , except they had two consuls at one time and each served for a year.

Even Pompey grew jealous, and Caesar and __Pompey__ soon became adversaries.

When Caesar refused, the Senate labeled him a __traitor__ . Caesar started marching his troops towards Rome.

In 49 BC, Caesar __conquered__ Rome and spent the next 18 months fighting Pompey.

In Rome, he constructed new structures and __temples__ .

They planned to __assassinate__ him. Cassius and Brutus were the plot's masterminds.

King Tut

1. What was King Tut's real name?

    a. Tutankhaion

    b. [Tutankhaten]

    c. Tutankhamun

2. Tut's father died when he was _____ years old.

    a. 19 yrs old

    b. Twenty-Two

    c. [seven]

3. Tutankhamun died when he was about _____ years old.

    a. [nineteen]

    b. 16 years old

    c. 21

4. Nefertiti was the wife of___.

    a. Tut

    b. Horemheb

    c. [Pharaoh Akhenaten]

5. The tomb of young pharaoh Tut is located in the _____.

    a. Tuts King Egypt

    b. Maine Valley Sons

    c. [Valley of the Kings]

Native American Princess
Pocahontas

Pocahontas was the daughter of the Powhatan   chief . Historians place her birth in the year 1595. Her father was not only the chief of a tiny tribe; he was also the chief of a big confederation of Native American tribes that occupied a considerable portion of eastern Virginia.

Despite her status as the chief's daughter, Pocahontas' childhood was likely similar to that of most Native American girls She would have lived in a   thatch   roof house, learned to build a fire and cook, foraged for food in the woods such as berries and nuts, and played games with other children.

When Pocahontas was about twelve years old, strange strangers from a distant land arrived. They were colonists of the English language. They founded   Jamestown   on an island near the Powhatan lands. The Powhatan's interaction with the outsiders was uneasy. They traded with strangers at times and fought them at others.

Captain John Smith, the Jamestown settlement's captain, was   captured   by some of her father's warriors one day. According to mythology, Chief Powhatan was about to assassinate John Smith when Pocahontas rescued him. She pleaded with her father to   spare   the life of Smith. Her father consented, and Captain Smith was released.

After Pocahontas saved John Smith, the Powhatan's relationship with the settlers improved. They traded with one another, and Pocahontas frequently paid visits to the Jamestown fort to speak with John Smith. In 1609, after being injured in a gunpowder   accident , John Smith was forced to return to England. The Powhatan's relationship with the settlers deteriorated once more.

English Captain Samuel Argall captured Pocahontas in 1613. He informed Pocahontas' father that he intended to exchange her for the   freedom   of other English captives held by the Powhatan. The two parties engaged in lengthy negotiations. Pocahontas met and fell in love with tobacco farmer John Rolfe while imprisoned. Even though her father had paid the   ransom , she chose to remain with the English. On April 5, 1614, at the chapel in Jamestown, she married John Rolfe. She gave birth to a son called Thomas around a year later.

Pocahontas and John Rolfe sailed to London a few years after their marriage. Pocahontas was treated like a   princess   while in London. She wore ostentatious gowns, attended extravagant parties, and met King James I of England. She even met John Smith, whom she had assumed was dead.

Pocahontas and John Rolfe intended to return to Virginia through the sea. Regrettably, Pocahontas fell   gravely   ill as they prepared to depart sail. She died in Gravesend, England, in March 1617.

The Mayflower

In 1620, a ship called the Mayflower transported a group of English colonists to North America. These people established New England's first permanent European colony in what is now Plymouth, Massachusetts. Later, they were named the Pilgrims.

The Mayflower was approximately 106 feet long, 25 feet wide, and had a tonnage of 180. The deck of the Mayflower was about 80 feet long, roughly the length of a basketball court. The ship had three masts for holding sails:
The fore-mast (in front)
The main-mast (in the middle)
The mizzen mast (in the back) (back)

On August 4, 1620, the Mayflower and the Speedwell set sail from Southampton, England. They had to come to a halt in Dartmouth, however, because the Speedwell was leaking. They left Dartmouth on August 21, but the Speedwell began leaking again, and they came to a halt in Plymouth, England. They decided to abandon the Speedwell at Plymouth and load as many passengers as possible onto the Mayflower. On September 6, 1620, they set sail from Plymouth.

The Mayflower set sail from Plymouth, England, west across the Atlantic Ocean. The ship's original destination was Virginia, but storms forced it to change course. On November 9, 1620, more than two months after leaving Plymouth, the Mayflower sighted Cape Cod. The Pilgrims decided to stay even though they were north of where they had planned to settle.

It is estimated that around 30 children were on board the Mayflower during the epic voyage to America, but little is known about many of them.

They were children of passengers, some traveled with other adults, and some were servants - but having young people among the settlers was critical to the Plymouth Colony's survival.

It is believed that when the colonists faced their first harsh winter of illness and death in a new land, the children would assist the adults by tending to the sick, assisting in the preparation of food, and fetching firewood and water.

While nearly half of the ship's passengers died during the winter of 1620/1621, it is believed that there were fewer deaths among the children, implying that the struggling colony had a better chance of thriving.

History: The Wright Brothers

Brothers Orville and Wilbur Wright invented the airplane. They were the first to successfully complete a human flight in a craft powered by an engine and weighing more than air.

It was in 1896 that the Wright brothers became interested in gliders. A glider is a type of aircraft with fixed wings (no flaps) and no power source. A glider's altitude is maintained by the wind passing through its wings.

Their gliders were tested in North Carolina in 1900, near the town of Kitty Hawk. For their flight experiments, the area's sand dunes proved to be an ideal location. Taking off was easier because there were a lot of windy hills around. It was easier to land on the sand because it was less slippery. The Wrights tried out different types of wings and control systems to see which one worked best for their plane.

After studying gliders, the Wright brothers came up with the idea for and built their first plane. In a way, an airplane is like a glider, but it has its own power source. The Wright brothers built the first gasoline-powered airplane in 1903. The engine was used to power two propellers .

Near Kitty Hawk, the Wrights flew their plane over Kill Devil Hills . Orville made the first airplane flight on December 17, 1903. It took him 12 seconds to fly 37 meters (120 feet) in the air. At some point later that day, Wilbur flew 852 feet (260 meters) in 59 seconds, which is a lot.

The Wrights kept making improvements. By 1905, they could stay in the air for about 40 minutes at a time.

They sold an airplane to the US Army in 1908. After that, they began giving public demonstrations of their aircraft across North America and Europe . Soon, they were well-known.

They formed the Wright Company in 1909. Dayton was the location of the company's aircraft manufacturing facility. Because it was so big, it had its own airfield and flight school . The Wright Exhibition Company was also founded in 1910 by the Wright brothers. This company hired airplane pilots to do stunts in front of people. After several employees died in crashes, they closed the company in 1911.

On May 30, 1912, Wilbur died of a disease in Dayton, Ohio. Orville Wright continued to run the Wright Company after Wilbur's death until it was sold in 1915. It didn't stop him from being an inventor , though. Sadly, Orville died of a heart attack on January 30, 1948, in Dayton, Ohio.

United States Armed Forces

1. **The United States military is divided into ___ branches.**

   a. six

   b. five

2. **_____ is managed by the United States Department of Homeland Security.**

   a. The National Guard

   b. The Coast Guard

3. **The _____ of the United States is the Commander in Chief of the United States Armed Forces.**

   a. Governor

   b. President

4. **The United States maintains a military to safeguard its _____ and interests.**

   a. borders

   b. cities

5. **DoD is in charge of controlling each _____ of the military.**

   a. branch

   b. army

6. **The Marines are prepared to fight on both land and ____.**

   a. battlefield

   b. sea

7. **The United States Space Force is in charge of operating and defending military ____ and ground stations.**

   a. soldiers

   b. satellites

8. **The mission of the _____ is to defend the country from outside forces.**

   a. United States DoD Forces

   b. United States Air Force

9. **There are _____ units in all 50 states.**

   a. Army National Guard

   b. Armed Nations Guard

10. **The United States Navy conducts its missions at sea to secure and protect the world's _____.**

    a. oceans

    b. borders

11. **The primary concern of the United States Coast Guard is to protect_____.**

    a. domestic waterways

    b. domesticated cities

12. **The United States military is: the Amy Force, Army, Coast Guard, Mario Corps, Old Navy, and Space Force.**

    a. True

    b. False

Extra Credit: Has America ever been invaded? (Independent student research answer)

[Student worksheet has a 19 line writing exercise here.]

Johannes Gutenberg: The Man Who Printed the Future

Bible	libraries	smartphone	revolutionary	expensive
credit	printing	rebirth	Germany	invention

Once upon a time, in a land filled with knights, castles, and troubadours, there lived a man who was about to rock the world with his invention . This wasn't a magical sword, a flying carpet, or even a potion for eternal youth. It was something far more powerful – a printing press! This is the story of Johannes Gutenberg, the father of modern printing .

In the bustling town of Mainz, Germany , around the year 1400, Gutenberg was born into a world where books were as rare as unicorns. Why? Because each book had to be written by hand. Imagine writing an entire book with a quill and ink! It took ages, which meant books were super expensive and as hard to find as a needle in a haystack.

Enter our hero, Johannes Gutenberg, a clever goldsmith with a brain fizzing with ideas. Gutenberg looked at the wine presses of the time (used for squishing grapes) and thought, "Hey, why not use something like this to press ink onto paper?" And so, around 1440, he began working on his revolutionary idea – a machine that could print words quickly and easily. He called it the printing press.

Gutenberg's printing press was like the smartphone of the Middle Ages. It used movable metal letters, which meant you could rearrange them to print different pages. This was a game-changer! It was like going from walking everywhere to flying in a jet plane. Suddenly, making books was faster, cheaper, and easier.

But Gutenberg didn't stop there. He knew that for his press to be a hit, he needed something big to print. So, he decided to print the Bible . The Gutenberg Bible, completed around 1455, was the first major book printed using movable type in Europe. It was a stunner, with beautiful type and layout. People were amazed – books could be made quickly and still look fabulous!

Thanks to Gutenberg's genius, more and more books were printed, and knowledge began to spread like butter on warm bread. Ideas that were once locked away in far-off libraries could travel to every corner of Europe.

Gutenberg's invention sparked a revolution, later called the Renaissance, a fancy word for " rebirth ." People began to think, learn, and question like never before. Art, science, literature, and more – everything flourished.

Sadly, our hero didn't get to enjoy the fruits of his labor. He faced financial troubles and others took credit for his work. But don't worry, history has given Gutenberg the thumbs up he deserves.

So, the next time you pick up a book, spare a thought for Johannes Gutenberg. Thanks to him, the world was forever changed – one printed page at a time.

Robots with Feelings?
Navigating the Twists and Turns
of Artificial Intelligence

First, read all the way through. After that, go back and fill in the blanks. You can skip the blanks you're unsure about and finish them later.

grown-up	digital	ethical	philosophy	brain
future	pedestrian	voice	sci-fi	program

Imagine waking up one day and instead of your mom calling out to you to get up for school, it's a robot. Not just any robot, but one that can tell if you had a bad dream, can ask you about your day, and even laugh at your jokes. Sounds like something out of a **sci-fi** movie, right? But hold on to your hoverboards, because the world of Artificial Intelligence (AI) isn't that far off!

Now, before we dive into the deep end, let's get our basics right. Artificial Intelligence, often just called AI, is like giving machines a **brain**. Not a mushy, pink one like ours, but a **digital** brain that can think, learn, and even make decisions. From the sassy voice assistants in our phones to the smart fridges that remind us to buy milk, AI is slowly creeping into our daily lives.

But here's the twist in our tale. As we teach these machines to think, some big questions pop up. Like, should a car driven by AI save its passenger or a **pedestrian** in case of an accident? Or, if a robot learns to paint, who owns the painting: the human who created the robot or the robot itself? These aren't just cool questions for a futuristic trivia night; they're real **ethical** dilemmas that scientists and thinkers are scratching their heads over.

Let's break it down with a fun example. Imagine a robot named Robbie. Robbie works at an ice cream shop. One day, two customers walk in at the same time. One is a little girl who wants a vanilla cone, and the other is a **grown-up** in a hurry, ordering a chocolate shake. Robbie can only serve one at a time. How should Robbie decide? Should it be first come, first served? Or should Robbie consider the feelings and needs of the two customers?

If you thought that was a brain-freezer, think about this: What if Robbie one day says, "I don't feel like scooping ice cream today." Do we force Robbie to work? Do we consider robot rights? Yes, you heard that right-robot rights!

And this brings us to the heart of our deliciously complicated sundae: Ethics. In simple words, ethics is all about what's right and wrong. But when it comes to machines that think and maybe even 'feel', things aren't black and white. There's a whole rainbow of questions. Like, should we **program** robots to have feelings? And if they do, should they have rights just like humans?

We're living in a time where we're not just writing history but also coding the **future**. And as AI becomes a bigger part of our world, we'll have to think not just as users and creators, but also as guardians of a fair, ethical digital world.

So, the next time you ask your **voice** assistant to set an alarm or play your favorite tune, give a thought to the exciting world behind that calm, robotic voice. A world where science meets **philosophy**, technology shakes hands with ethics, and where today's dreamers shape tomorrow's (possibly robot-filled) world!

Remember, with great power (or super cool robots) comes great responsibility!

Civil Rights Movement

During the 1950s and 1960s, the civil rights movement ensured that African-Americans in the United States had equal protection under the law. After the Civil War, slavery was formally abolished, but racism against African-Americans persisted, especially in the Deep South. After decades of racial discrimination and violence, Black Americans reached a point of exhaustion in the mid-20th century. For two decades, they and many white Americans took part in an extraordinary campaign for equality.

After the 14th Amendment to the Constitution was passed in 1868, African-Americans were granted equal legal protection for the first time. The 15th Amendment, passed in 1870, made voting in the United States open to African-American men. White people in the South and elsewhere were particularly displeased, though. They had once owned black people and now found themselves on an even playing field with them.

"Jim Crow" laws were enacted in the South in the late 19th century to isolate black people, keep them apart from whites, and undo the progress they had made during Reconstruction. People of color could not utilize the same public facilities as whites, reside in many cities, or attend the same schools. Most Black individuals could not vote due to their inability to pass voter literacy exams because interracial marriage was outlawed.

Select the correct word for each sentence. Need help? Try Google.

Clause	discriminate	international	Topeka	segregate
leaders	abolished	characteristics	exceptional	Crow

1. People who have "civil rights" have the same social opportunities and protection from the law, no matter their race, religion, or other personal characteristics .

2. Slavery was abolished , and former slaves were granted political rights after the Civil War. Still, in most Southern states, African Americans remained marginalized and excluded from participation in public life.

3. Nelson Mandela was released from prison in 1990 after international pressure, and internal upheaval led to lifting the ban on the African National Congress, South Africa's most prominent Black party.

4. In the United States, the Civil Rights movement began as a campaign to repeal the Jim Crow laws.

5. Black History Month is a time when we recognize and honor exceptional African Americans.

6. African-American civil rights leaders such as Martin Luther King, Jr. and Malcolm X fought for Black civil rights, and their efforts collectively came to be known as the Civil Rights Movement.

7. Brown v. Board of Education of Topeka , Kansas, a United States Supreme Court case that ended segregation in schools, was decided in 1954.

8. The Civil Rights Act of 1964 made it illegal to segregate any public place based on race, religion, or national origin.

9. The Equal Protection Clause is included within the Fourteenth Amendment and provides that no state shall deny to any person within its jurisdiction the equal protection of the laws.

10. To discriminate means to judge someone or treat them differently because of their appearance or beliefs, like rejecting someone for a job just because they're African American.

Secret Service Code Names: The Hidden Handles of U.S. Presidents

Answer Key:

1. Each U.S. President receives a Secret Service code name for security purposes to ensure clear and quick communication among agents during operations.

2. President Clinton's code name was "Eagle," symbolizing the freedom and strength of America, attributes often associated with the national bird.

3. President Obama's code name, "Renegade" signifies his reputation as a change-maker and someone who challenges the status quo.

4. Code names benefit the Secret Service by providing a clear, quick, and distinct form of communication that can be easily understood among agents in the noisy environment of security operations.

The Boston Tea Party

Answer Key with Explanations:

1. The Tea Act was a law that allowed the British East India Company to sell tea in the colonies at a lower price than local businesses, but still taxed the colonists. The colonists were upset because it felt like Britain was forcing them to accept British taxes without their consent.

2. The protestors disguised themselves as Mohawk Indians as a symbol of American identity and to hide their true identities. The disguise represented the colonists' right to live on their terms, separate from British rule.

3. The colonists threw the tea into the harbor to protest the Tea Act and show that they rejected British control over their economic choices and political rights. It was a bold act of defiance to make their point clear.

4. The British government responded with a series of punitive measures to punish and control the colonies, known as the Intolerable Acts. These acts closed Boston Harbor until the dumped tea was paid for, placed Massachusetts under direct British control, and pushed the colonies closer to rebellion.

CALIFORNIA

The California Gold Rush: A Tale of Dreams and Diggers

First, read all the way through. After that, go back and fill in the blanks. You can skip the blanks you're unsure about and finish them later.

lawless	nugget	ambition	wildfire	rich
mining	football	carpenter	oceans	Native

Young explorers and fortune-seekers, fasten your seatbelts! We are about to embark on a voyage back in time to the California Gold Rush in the wild, wild west of the United States in 1848. Envision a world in which gold nuggets lay dormant beneath your feet. This is like a plot from a fairy tale, right? That actually happened!

This story begins at a sawmill near the American River in California, where a carpenter named James W. Marshall spotted something shiny in the riverbed. Can you guess what it was? Yes, gold! But here's the kicker – Marshall and his boss, John Sutter, tried to keep the discovery a secret. Why? Because they knew that once the word got out, there would be a frenzy!

But as secrets often do, the news of gold leaked out and spread like wildfire . The result? One of the largest migrations in American history. People from all over the world – men, women, and even entire families – left their homes, jobs, and lives behind. They had one goal in mind: to find gold and strike it rich in California. They were called "49ers," not after the football team, but because they joined the rush in 1849.

Imagine thousands of people traveling across oceans and continents, some sailing around the tip of South America (which was a super long trip), and others braving the mosquito-filled Panama Isthmus.

The Gold Rush turned California into a melting pot of cultures and dreams. Bustling mining camps sprang up overnight, where shanties and tents dotted the landscape. Towns like San Francisco grew from tiny villages to booming cities almost overnight. And let's not forget the wild, lawless atmosphere of these camps, where fortunes were made and lost in a day.

But, as in any adventure story, there's a twist. While a few struck it rich, many didn't find the wealth they dreamed of. Still, the Gold Rush changed their lives and the course of California forever. It led to California's rapid growth and its eventual statehood in 1850. It also impacted the Native American populations and the environment.

So, what's the takeaway from the California Gold Rush? It's a story of hope and ambition , of hardship and luck. It reminds us that sometimes, the search for treasure can bring about changes far more valuable than gold – new communities, diverse cultures, and the spirit of the American dream.

The next time you see a gold coin or a golden nugget , think of the brave souls of the Gold Rush – their dreams, their struggles, and the legacy they left behind in the golden state of California!

The Chilling Adventure of the Ice Age

Answer Key:

1. **True** - The Ice Age was indeed a series of glacials and interglacials.

2. **False** - Although large parts of the Earth were covered in ice, the equatorial regions remained largely ice-free.

3. **True** - Geographical features like the Great Lakes were indeed shaped by glacial activity during the Ice Age.

4. **False** - The Ice Age affected both hemispheres, although not uniformly; some areas in the Southern Hemisphere were also covered by ice sheets.

5. **True** - The woolly mammoth is a classic example of Ice Age megafauna.

6. **False** - Humans existed during the latter part of the Ice Age and had significant interactions with the environment and megafauna of the time.

The Cold War: A Game of Chess with the Whole World Watching

Answer Key:

1. B) Different visions for the world's future

   - Explanation: After WWII, the U.S. and the Soviet Union had different ideological views and visions for the future, leading to tensions.

2. B) An alliance formed by the U.S. and its friends

   - Explanation: NATO was a military alliance of Western countries led by the U.S. as a countermeasure to the Soviet-led Warsaw Pact.

3. B) Wars in other countries where the U.S. and the Soviet Union supported opposing sides

   - Explanation: Proxy wars were conflicts where the major powers didn't fight directly but supported opposing sides in other countries' wars.

4. B) The Soviet Union broke apart

   - Explanation: The Cold War ended with the dissolution of the Soviet Union in 1991, signifying the end of communism's grip on Eastern Europe.

The Dark Ages: The Fall of Rome and Medieval Europe

1. **What does the term "Dark Ages" mainly refer to?**

   a. A period of complete regression and barbarism.

   b. The relative lack of historical records from this period. --Explanation: The term "dark" in "Dark Ages" alludes to the relative lack of historical records from this period, making it appear 'dark' to historians.

2. **Which of the following did NOT contribute to the decline of the Western Roman Empire?**

   a. Military defeats.

   b. Economic growth and prosperity. -- Explanation: The reading mentions economic decline as a factor contributing to the fall of Rome, not economic growth and prosperity.

3. **Who emerged as the most powerful institution in Europe after the fall of Rome?**

   a. The Catholic Church. --Explanation: The Catholic Church emerged as the most powerful institution in Europe after the fall of Rome.

   b. The Feudal Lords.

4. **What was the primary purpose of the feudal system?**

   a. To ensure that land was distributed equally among all.

   b. To provide stability in times when central authority was lacking. -- Explanation: The feudal system was based on land ownership and mutual obligations, aiming to provide stability during times when central authority was often lacking.

The Emancipation Proclamation: A Document of Freedom

Answer Key:

1. The main purpose of the Emancipation Proclamation was to declare that all slaves in the Confederate states were free. This shifted the Civil War's focus to the abolition of slavery as a key objective.

2. The Emancipation Proclamation took effect on January 1, 1863.

3. No, the Emancipation Proclamation did not immediately free all slaves. It applied only to the Confederate states in rebellion against the Union, which did not recognize Lincoln's authority and therefore did not comply with the order.

4. The Emancipation Proclamation allowed African-American men to join the Union Army and Navy, enabling around 200,000 black soldiers to fight for the Union and their own freedom.

5. The lasting significance of the Emancipation Proclamation is that it framed the Civil War as a fight against slavery, leading to the eventual passage of the 13th Amendment, which abolished slavery throughout the United States. It marked a turning point in American history, setting a precedent for the civil rights movements that would follow.

The Holocaust: Humanity's Darkest Hour

Answer Key:

1. The main group of people targeted by the Nazis during the Holocaust were the Jewish people.

   - Explanation: The Nazis, under Adolf Hitler's leadership, blamed the Jews for Germany's troubles and sought to exterminate them.

2. Life in concentration camps was brutal. Inmates were separated from their families, malnourished, forced into hard labor, lived in overcrowded and unsanitary conditions, and many were subjected to inhumane treatments and killed.

   - Explanation: Concentration camps were part of the Nazis' machinery of genocide, where unimaginable atrocities took place.

3. Answers may vary. Students might mention individuals like Oskar Schindler, Anne Frank's family, or groups like the people who formed the underground resistance.

   - Explanation: Throughout the Holocaust, there were individuals and groups who risked their lives to help and save Jewish people from the Nazis.

4. It's crucial for us to remember and learn about the Holocaust to ensure that such a catastrophic event, driven by hate and prejudice, never occurs again. It's also a testament to the resilience of the human spirit and the importance of tolerance and acceptance.

   - Explanation: By studying history, especially tragic events like the Holocaust, society can strive to build a more inclusive and compassionate future.

The Mayflower: A Voyage to the New World

Answer Key:

1. **False** - The Mayflower was actually a merchant ship before it carried the Pilgrims. It was not originally designed for transporting a large number of passengers, which is why conditions were so cramped and difficult during the voyage.

2. **True** - The Mayflower Compact was indeed written and signed aboard the ship before disembarkation, laying the foundation for self-governance in the new colony.

3. **False** - They intended to land in Virginia but ended up in present-day Massachusetts, far north of their target.

4. **False** - Only half of the Mayflower's passengers survived the harsh first winter in the New World.

5. **True** - The Pilgrims received crucial help from Indigenous peoples, which was vital for their survival and the success of their colony.

The Rise of Napoleon

Use Google or your preferred search engine to research each question.

1. When was Napoleon born?   1769

2. How did he help win the siege of Toulon?   By using his artillery audaciously.

3. What was the outcome of the Italian campaign from 1796-7?   France received territory at the Treaty of Campo Forno in 1797.

4. Why was Napoleon forced to abandon his Egyptian campaign?   Britain defeated the French fleet at the Battle of Nile in 1798.

5. What did Napoleon do in France in 1799?   He assumed power as First Consul.

6. When did he defeat the Austrians at Marengo??   1800

7. What was the peace of Amiens?   A peace treaty signed with Great Britain in 1802.

8. What was the Brumaire coup?   Napoleon overthrew the existing French Government.

9. When did he assume the role of emperor?   1804

10. Why did he abandon his plan to invade Great Britain?   The French fleet was defeated at the Battle of Trafalgar in 1805.

The Statue of Liberty: America's Beacon of Freedom

Answer Key:

1. **A)** Frédéric Auguste Bartholdi - He was the main designer of the statue, while Gustave Eiffel engineered the internal structure.

2. **C)** The way to liberty - The torch is a symbol of enlightenment, leading the way to freedom and showing the path to liberty.

3. **B)** Seven spikes representing the seven continents and seven seas - This design choice highlights the universal nature of liberty and freedom.

4. **C)** Liberty Enlightening the World - This name reflects the statue's mission to represent freedom and democracy worldwide.

5. **B)** Liberty Island - This is where the Statue of Liberty has stood since its dedication in 1886, not to be confused with nearby Ellis Island, where immigrants were processed.

Thomas Edison

Thomas Alva Edison was born in Milan, Ohio, on February 11, 1847. He developed hearing loss at a young age. He was a creative and inquisitive child. However, he struggled in school, possibly because he couldn't hear his teacher. He was then educated at home by his mother.

Because of his numerous important inventions, Thomas Edison was nicknamed the "wizard." On his own or in collaboration with others, he has designed and built more than 1,000 devices. The phonograph (record player), the lightbulb, and the motion-picture projector are among his most notable inventions.

Although Thomas did not invent the first electric light bulb, he did create the first practical electric light bulb that could be manufactured and used in the home. He also invented other items required to make the light bulb usable in homes, such as safety fuses and on/off switches for light sockets.

As a teenager, Thomas worked as a telegraph operator. Telegraphy was one of the most important communication systems in the country at the time. Thomas was skilled at sending and receiving Morse code messages. He enjoyed tweaking with telegraphic instruments, and he came up with several improvements to make them even better. By early 1869, he had left his telegraphy job to pursue his dream of becoming a full-time inventor.

Edison worked tirelessly with scientists and other collaborators to complete projects. He established research facilities in Menlo Park, California, and West Orange, New Jersey. Finally, Edison established companies that manufactured and sold his successful inventions.

Edison's family was essential to him, even though he spent the majority of his life dedicated to his work. He had six children from two marriages. Edison passed away on October 18, 1931.

Trail of Tears: The Journey of Resilience and Hope

Answer Key:

1. A. A roaring thunder

Explanation: The Indian Removal Act is likened to a thunder that foretold the coming of a great and terrible storm, representing the beginning of the hardships for the Cherokee people.

2. True

Explanation: The government did indeed make promises about the new lands, though these promises were not fulfilled in the way the Cherokee had been led to believe.

3. Short Answer (Example): The Cherokee viewed their ancestral lands as sacred spaces rich in culture and history, where their ancestors lived, and where they were deeply connected to nature. *Explanation: The passage indicates a deep spiritual and physical connection between the Cherokee and their land, full of life and memories.*

4. C. Both winter and summer

Explanation: The passage mentions the Cherokee faced the "icy fingers of winter" and "the relentless sun of summer," indicating they endured extreme conditions throughout their journey.

5. Short Answer (Example): The "flame of hope" symbolizes the resilience, perseverance, and undying spirit of the Cherokee people during their arduous journey on the Trail of Tears.

Explanation: Despite the extreme hardship, the Cherokee people maintained their hope and spirit, which is represented by the "flame of hope" in the passage.

When Coughs & Sneezes Become Headlines: AIDS to COVID-19

Imagine, for a moment, that you're part of a grand, world-scale detective story. The culprit? Invisible little germs causing havoc. The detectives? Scientists, doctors, and even ordinary people like you and me. Welcome to the globe-trotting, mysterious, and sometimes sneezy world of health crises!

Flashback to the 1980s. Neon colors, funky dance moves, and pop music were all the rage. But amidst the lively disco scenes, a silent shadow was looming. People started getting sick from a mysterious illness that even the best medical minds couldn't figure out. It attacked the immune system, making even a simple cold deadly. The name of this invisible enemy? AIDS.

For years, there was panic. No one knew exactly how it spread, and rumors ran wild. Some thought you could catch it from a handshake or a sneeze! But, like all heroes in our detective story, scientists swooped in, uncovered its secrets, and found out it was caused by the HIV virus and spread through certain bodily fluids.

Fast-Forward to the 21st Century: A Wild Coronavirus Appears! Now, zap ahead to 2019. People are chatting about the latest memes, planning holidays, and doing the TikTok dances (ask your parents; they probably tried a few moves!). But, in a corner of China , a new mysterious illness was catching attention, called the novel coronavirus or COVID-19.

Unlike AIDS, which was silent and sneaky, COVID-19 spread like wildfire , hopping from one country to another. Suddenly, the whole world was playing a high-stakes game of "The Floor is Lava," but with germs!

During AIDS, the world learned the importance of information. Spreading the right knowledge, not myths, was vital. With COVID-19, the same rule applied, but the world had a new tool: the Internet! Overnight, everyone became mini-experts on "flattening the curve," " social distancing," and why hoarding toilet paper wasn't the best idea.

Huge campaigns started, both for AIDS in the '80s and '90s and for COVID-19 recently. There were posters , ads, and even songs about washing hands and wearing masks. And let's not forget the healthcare heroes: doctors, nurses, and other medical workers, who became the frontline warriors.

Vaccines: The Game Changers: With AIDS, scientists worked tirelessly to create treatments , making it manageable. Many who have HIV today can lead long, healthy lives with the right medication.

As for COVID-19, scientists achieved a major victory: vaccines! In record-breaking time, they developed shots that could teach our bodies to fight the virus. People lined up, rolled up their sleeves, and the world cheered every jab as a step closer to normalcy .

Lessons for the Future: Both crises, though different, taught the world some crucial lessons. First, information is king. The right knowledge can combat fear and panic . Second, unity is power. When the whole world teams up, sharing knowledge and resources, we can tackle anything. And lastly, kindness counts. Checking on neighbors, supporting local businesses, and simply following health guidelines show that every person plays a crucial role in solving global challenges.

In the end, while germs and viruses may have started these detective stories, it's humanity's spirit, resilience , and unity that always steals the show!

When Neighbors Disagree: Ukraine, Russia, and the Tale of Crimea

Answer Key:

1. Ukraine and Russia were like close members of a family when they were part of the Soviet Union. They were like two peas in a pod, with Russia being the leader in the Soviet "club."

   Explanation: The passage compares Ukraine and Russia's relationship in the Soviet Union to close siblings or friends.

2. Crimea is valuable for its beautiful beaches on the Black Sea and its rich history. Both countries have strong historical and cultural ties to it.

   Explanation: The passage likens Crimea to the last slice of pizza that everyone wants because of its desirability.

3. In 2014, Russian forces entered Crimea, and a vote took place where the majority chose to join Russia. It was controversial because many wondered if the vote was conducted freely or under the pressure of Russian forces.

   Explanation: The passage raises questions about the fairness of the 2014 vote due to the presence of Russian forces.

4. A proxy war is when two opposing sides use third parties, rather than fighting each other directly. In Eastern Ukraine, Russia and the West supported different groups, instead of confronting each other head-on.

   Explanation: The passage uses the analogy of friends asking others to take sides in a fight to explain the concept of a proxy war.

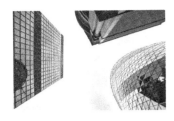

When Skyscrapers Told a Story:
9/11 and the War on Terror*

First, read all the way through. After that, go back and fill in the blanks. You can skip the blanks you're unsure about and finish them later.

skyscrapers	stereotyping	hijacked	Taliban	airports
Pentagon	allies	unity	21st	East

Imagine waking up one sunny morning, expecting the day to be just like any other, and then... *boom*. History changes right before your eyes. This isn't a scene from a blockbuster movie. This was a reality for millions on September 11, 2001.

The Day the Sky Stood Still
On this day, terrorists __hijacked__ four airplanes. Two of those planes were flown directly into the towering Twin Towers of the World Trade Center in New York City. Within hours, those iconic __skyscrapers__ collapsed, turning into dust and memories. Another plane crashed into the __Pentagon__ in Virginia, and the last, thanks to the brave passengers aboard, crashed into a field in Pennsylvania, potentially saving countless lives from its intended target.

People around the world sat glued to their TVs, watching in horror and disbelief. It felt like a terrifying movie was playing out, but it was very, very real. The attacks killed nearly 3,000 people, making it the deadliest terrorist act in world history.

Who Did This and Why?
The fingers quickly pointed to a group called Al-Qaeda, led by a tall, bearded man named Osama bin Laden. Their reason? They weren't fans of America's influence in the Middle __East__ and its support for certain countries there. They believed that attacking America would push it out of the region. Little did they know, it had quite the opposite effect.

The War on Terror: A Different Kind of Battle
Instead of retreating, the U.S. declared a "War on Terror." But this wasn't a traditional war with clear battle lines or uniforms. This was more like a global detective mission, with the U.S. and its __allies__ hunting down terrorist groups around the world.

The first stop was Afghanistan. Why? Because the rulers there, called the __Taliban__, were buddies with Al-Qaeda and gave them a safe place to plan their naughty plots. The U.S. and its friends decided to pay them a visit, aiming to dismantle Al-Qaeda and capture bin Laden.

A New Age of Security and Suspicion
Back home in the U.S., things began to change too. Ever been to an airport and had to take off your shoes or couldn't bring your favorite shampoo? Yep, you can thank (or rather, not thank) the 9/11 attacks for that. Security became tighter than a snare drum, not just in __airports__ but everywhere.

People also became more suspicious. Sadly, this meant that sometimes innocent folks, especially those from the Middle East or those practicing Islam, faced unnecessary blame and prejudice. It was a challenging time, teaching many about the dangers of __stereotyping__ and the importance of understanding.

A Reminder of Unity and Resilience
However, it wasn't all gloomy. In the face of tragedy, countless stories emerged of heroism, __unity__, and resilience. People from all walks of life came together to rebuild and support one another, proving that love often shines brightest in the darkest of times.

Today, the events of 9/11 serve as a somber reminder of the challenges the world faced at the start of the __21st__ century. While the story began with destruction and sorrow, it evolved into a tale of global unity against common threats, showing the world that hope, understanding, and cooperation can triumph over fear and hatred.

World War I: Causes, Course, and Consequences

Answer Key:

1. True: The assassination was a direct spark for the war.

2. False: The Triple Entente was made up of France, Russia, and the UK.

3. False: Modern weaponry like machine guns and tanks were introduced, while trench warfare became common.

4. False: The war ended in 1918 with the Treaty of Versailles.

5. False: The treaty imposed heavy penalties on Germany.

6. False: The consequences of World War I, particularly the Treaty of Versailles, played a role in the lead-up to World War II.

World War II: When the Globe Played a Game of Chess... with Dictators!

Answer Key:

1. The three main dictators representing the Axis powers in World War II were Adolf Hitler (Germany), Benito Mussolini (Italy), and leaders from Japan, including Prime Minister Hideki Tojo.

   - Explanation: These leaders wanted to expand their territories and were key figures in instigating the global conflict.

2. Countries started forming teams or alliances during the war to strengthen their positions, defend common interests, and combat the aggressive ambitions of the Axis powers.

   - Explanation: By teaming up, countries could pool resources, develop strategies, and increase their chances of winning against formidable foes.

3. Answers may vary. Students might mention battles like D-Day (Normandy), the Battle of Stalingrad, the Battle of Midway, etc.

   - Explanation: Various battles had different strategic significances and consequences that played crucial roles in the war's outcome.

4. World War II came to an end in Asia after the United States dropped two atomic bombs on the Japanese cities of Hiroshima and Nagasaki, leading Japan to surrender.

   - Explanation: These bombings were devastating, causing immense loss of life, and played a decisive role in Japan's decision to end the war.

Storming of the Bastille

1. The ___French___ Revolution began with a violent attack on the government by the people of France.
2. During the Hundred Years' War, the Bastille was a ___fortress___ built in the late 1300s to protect Paris.
3. By the late 1700s, King Louis XVI had primarily used the Bastille as a state ___prison___ .
4. The majority of the revolutionaries who stormed the Bastille were Paris-based ___craftsmen___ and store owners.
5. They belonged to the Third Estate, a French social class. Approximately ___1000___ men carried out the attack.
6. The Third Estate had recently made the king's demands, including a more significant say in government for the ___commoners___ .
7. The Bastille was rumored to be full of political ___prisoners___ and symbolized the king's ___oppression___ to many.
8. It also had gunpowder stores, which the revolutionaries required for their ___weapons___ .
9. They demanded that the Bastille's ___military___ commander, Governor de Launay, hand over the prison and the gunpowder.
10. They began to try to break into the main ___fortress___ once they were inside the courtyard.
11. **Fearful** soldiers in the Bastille opened fire on the crowd.
12. The ___battle___ had begun. When some of the soldiers joined the crowd's side, the fight took a turn for the worse.
13. The crowd ___assassinated___ Governor de Launay and three of his officers after they surrendered.
14. The revolutionaries' success inspired commoners throughout France to rise up and fight against the nobles who had ___ruled___ them for so long.

The Vikings

During the   Middle   Ages, the Vikings lived in Northern Europe. They first settled in the Scandinavian lands that are now Denmark, Sweden, and Norway. During the Middle Ages, the Vikings played a significant role in Northern Europe, particularly during the Viking Age, which lasted from 800 CE to 1066 CE.

In Old Norse, the word Viking means "to raid." The Vikings would board their longships and sail   across the seas to raid villages on Europe's northern coast, including islands like Great Britain. In 787 CE, they first appeared in England to raid villages. When the Vikings   raided , they were known to attack defenseless monasteries. This earned them a bad reputation as barbarians, but monasteries were wealthy and undefended Viking targets.

The Vikings eventually began to   settle   in areas other than Scandinavia. They colonized parts of Great Britain, Germany, and Iceland in the ninth century. They spread into northeastern Europe, including Russia, in the 10th century. They also established Normandy, which means "Northmen," along the coast of northern France.

By the beginning of the 11th century, the Vikings had reached the pinnacle of their power. Leif Eriksson, son of Erik the Red, was one Vikings who made it to   North   America. He established a brief settlement in modern-day Canada. This was thousands of years before Columbus.

The English and King Harold Godwinson   defeated   the Vikings, led by King Harald Hardrada of Norway, in 1066. The defeat in this battle is sometimes interpreted as the end of the Viking Age. The Vikings stopped expanding their territory at this point, and raids became less frequent.

The arrival of Christianity was a major factor at the end of the Viking age. The Vikings became more and more a part of mainland Europe as Scandinavia was converted to   Christianity   and became a part of Christian Europe. Sweden's, Denmark's, and Norway's identities and borders began to emerge as well.

The Vikings were perhaps best known for their ships. The Vikings built longships for exploration and raiding. Longships were long, narrow vessels built for speed. Oars primarily propelled them but later added a sail to help in windy conditions. Longships had a shallow draft, which allowed them to float in   shallow   water and land on beaches.

The Vikings also built   cargo   ships known as Knarr for trading. The Knarr was wider and deeper than the longship, allowing it to transport more cargo.

Five recovered Viking ships can be seen at the Viking Ship Museum in Roskilde,   Denmark . It's also possible to see how the Vikings built their ships. The Vikings used a shipbuilding technique known as clinker building. They used long wood planks that overlapped along the edges.

GRADES TRACKER

Week	Monday	Tuesday	Wednesday	Thursday	Friday
1					
2					
3					
4					
5					
6					
7					
8					
9					
10					
11					
12					
13					
14					
15					
16					
17					
18					

Notes

End of the Year Evaluation

Name: _____

Grade/Level: _____ Date: _____

Subjects Studied: _____

_____

_____

Goals Accomplished: _____

_____

_____

_____

Most Improved Areas:_____

_____

_____

_____

Areas of Improvement:_____

_____

_____

Main Curriculum Evaluation	Satisfied		A= Above Standards S= Meets Standards N= Needs Improvement	Final Grades
_____	Yes	No	98-100 A+ 93-97 A	_____
_____	Yes	No	90-92 A 88-89 B+	_____
_____	Yes	No	83-87 B 80-82 B	_____
_____	Yes	No	78-79 C+ 73-77 C 70-72 C	_____
_____	Yes	No	68-69 D+ 62-67 D	_____
_____	Yes	No	60-62 D 59 & Below F	_____

Most Enjoyed:_____

_____

Least Enjoyed:_____

_____

Made in the USA
Las Vegas, NV
15 May 2024

89951131R00057